WATERFALL HIKES
IN SOUTHERN BRITISH COLUMBIA

STEVE TERSMETTE

WATERFALL
in Southern British Columbia
HIKES

RMB

For information on purchasing bulk quantities of this book, or to obtain media excerpts or invite the author to speak at an event, please visit rmbooks.com and select the "Contact" tab.

RMB | Rocky Mountain Books Ltd.
rmbooks.com
@rmbooks
facebook.com/rmbooks

Cataloguing data available from Library and Archives Canada
ISBN 9781771604277 (paperback)
ISBN 9781771604284 (electronic)

All photographs are by Steve Tersmette unless otherwise noted.

Printed and bound in China

We would like to also take this opportunity to acknowledge the traditional territories upon which we live and work. In Calgary, Alberta, we acknowledge the Niitsítapi (Blackfoot) and the people of the Treaty 7 region in Southern Alberta, which includes the Siksika, the Piikuni, the Kainai, the Tsuut'ina and the Stoney Nakoda First Nations, including Chiniki, Bearpaw, and Wesley First Nations. The City of Calgary is also home to Métis Nation of Alberta, Region III. In Victoria, British Columbia, we acknowledge the traditional territories of the Lkwungen (Esquimalt, and Songhees), Malahat, Pacheedaht, Scia'new, T'Sou-ke and WSÁNEĆ (Pauquachin, Tsartlip, Tsawout, Tseycum) peoples.

We acknowledge the financial support of the Government of Canada through the Canada Book Fund and the Canada Council for the Arts, and of the province of British Columbia through the British Columbia Arts Council and the Book Publishing Tax Credit.

DISCLAIMER

The actions described in this book may be considered inherently dangerous activities. Individuals undertake these activities at their own risk. The information put forth in this guide has been collected from a variety of sources and is not guaranteed to be completely accurate or reliable. Many conditions and some information may change owing to weather and numerous other factors beyond the control of the authors and publishers. Individuals or groups must determine the risks, use their own judgment, and take full responsibility for their actions. Do not depend on any information found in this book for your own personal safety. Your safety depends on your own good judgment based on your skills, education, and experience.

It is up to the users of this guidebook to acquire the necessary skills for safe experiences and to exercise caution in potentially hazardous areas. The authors and publishers of this guide accept no responsibility for your actions or the results that occur from another's actions, choices, or judgments. If you have any doubt as to your safety or your ability to attempt anything described in this guidebook, do not attempt it.

For Hanna and Jasper

Contents

Foreword

I met Steve Tersmette on a backpacking trip along the Rockwall Trail in Kootenay National Park back in 2018. We talked about many things during the drive to the trailhead, including our mutual love and admiration of waterfalls. I had never witnessed a real waterfall in person until my first drive along the Oregon side of the Columbia River Gorge when I moved to Portland 15 years ago. I became instantly enamored. Beyond the allure for the senses of hearing and sight, cascades draw us to them on a primal level. Something deep within us knows that a waterfall is a potential source of food and water. And depending on how far down the rabbit hole you want to go, there are claims that the negative ions produced by the crashing water act as a mood boost when we breathe in the air that surrounds them. It wasn't long after that first trip that the Columbia River Gorge became my favourite place in the world.

So when we passed Columbia Lake, the headwaters of the namesake river and gorge I so covet, I was giddy. As we drove by I mentioned to Steve how excited I was to be seeing it. Steve then informed me that Dutch Creek is the longest stream that feeds Columbia Lake. He had traced Dutch Creek to its primary feeder stream and followed that to its source – a muddy trickle from a remnant glacier on the northeast face of Trikootenay Peak, high in the Purcell Mountains – simply to see the very origin of the Columbia River. At that moment, eyes wide and mouth agape, I knew that Steve Tersmette was a fella I wanted to know. He sees the natural world with a fascination and reverence that very few possess.

I picked his brain almost ceaselessly over the next five days in an attempt to learn as much about the wilderness of British Columbia as I possibly could. And he happily obliged, providing information with uncommonly thoughtful and balanced insight. At the time, Steve was just getting his feet wet with writing about the outdoors, and I recognized it was only a matter of time before he would get one of those feet into a major door. And here we are. It's an honor to introduce Steve Tersmette to the guidebook-reading public. I'm sure you'll enjoy his knowledge, writing and photography as much as I do.

—Adam Sawyer, professional gentleman of leisure, author of *Hiking Waterfalls Oregon* and *Hiking Waterfalls Idaho*; co-author of *Hiking Waterfalls Washington*

Introduction

I was that kid: pressed against the back window of the family van searching for roadside cascades as we made our way west for an annual summer camping trip. Every single little stream that poured out of the mountains gave rise to a backseat celebration before we reset our eyes, hoping to catch another fleeting glimpse of the next waterfall. Not much has changed. I am still that kid, although now, as the driver, it is slightly more dangerous to be on the lookout for waterfalls while negotiating the Formula One racetrack that the Trans-Canada Highway has become.

The captivating force that attracts people to waterfalls is nothing less than magical. From small hypnotic cascades delicately bubbling over rocks and tree limbs to the deafening roar of a swollen river rocketing over a cliff, people go to great lengths to seek out these natural wonders. Waterfalls provide an escape, a solace for the mind while soothing the soul. And they are pretty things to photograph.

The purpose of this book is to provide a simple, family-friendly hiking guide as an aid in locating and accessing the spectacular waterfalls in southern British Columbia. This comprehensive guide details nearly a hundred waterfalls, encompassing the area south of the Trans-Canada corridor in the north, to the Alberta and US borders to the east and south, and to the Highway 97 corridor in the west.

First and foremost I want to thank my wife, Katie, and our two children, Hanna and Jasper, for being such great sports as we hunted waterfalls at every opportunity. I want to thank Adam Sawyer for inspiring me to get writing, for the idea of creating this guidebook and for ecstatically providing the foreword. To my good friend Robin and sister-in-law Tawny for reading, rereading and surgically editing draft after draft of this literary masterpiece. To my father for instilling in me a deep-seated and insatiable love for mountains, hiking and the outdoors. To my many climbing partners over the years who continue to fuel my passion and whose own accomplishments never cease to amaze. To Meghan Ward at Crowfoot Media for giving me a shot. And finally, to Don Gorman at Rocky Mountain Books for his excitement for this project; his guidance and professionalism have been critical in bringing the project to fruition.

Writing this book not only kept us hiking and exploring together as a family but also filled a much needed void in the guidebook genre: kid-friendly exploration. Oh, and did I mention? It's about waterfalls!

Using the guidebook

This comprehensive, simple and family-friendly hiking guide will aid readers in locating and accessing the spectacular waterfalls of southern British Columbia. While every measure has been taken to ensure the accuracy of driving and hiking directions, even the most competent of writers have mashed buttons on their keyboard at some point. If you discover an error, please inform the author and publisher so that potential future printings can be updated.

Trail difficulty ratings

There are a variety of trails described herein, from five-minute walks out your car door, to destinations that may require a night out in a tent. Difficulty ratings are highly subjective and depend on the reader's experience, comfort and fitness level. The trails are rated with a family in mind, including younger children who can walk on a hiking trail on their own. My kids were six and eight years old during the construction of this guidebook and therefore served as the measuring stick for hiking times and difficulty. Read trail descriptions carefully to assess whether a hike might or might not be within your wheelhouse.

Trail difficulty can vary depending on conditions, time of day, season, weather, precipitation and temperature. Hike at your own risk and make smart decisions based on your skill level and experience. Even hiking on well-used trails has its hazards, such as roots, rocks and mud. Another thing to keep in mind is that waterfalls tend to get things pretty wet. Spray can travel for dozens of metres, making the areas around waterfalls slippery and dangerous, even with good footwear.

- Easy Less than half a day. One-way distance of less than 3 km or 1 hour on well-defined and well-marked trails with relatively minor elevation gains.
- Moderate A half-day to a full-day hike. Between 3 and 5 km one way with modest elevation gains or undulating terrain. Might also include shorter hikes with sustained steep or narrow sections.
- Difficult Requires a long day or an overnight trip. Might have significant elevation gains. Potential hazards may include difficult-to-follow trails, creek crossings or steep terrain. Pay careful attention to trail descriptions.

Getting there

While many trails are readily accessible from a highway, some are approachable only by forestry service roads (FSRs). British Columbians are blessed with an abundance of this infrastructure. Some forestry roads are well maintained for industrial or recreational purposes, while others fall into disrepair or go years without the benefit of maintenance. Access difficulty is described for a two wheel drive vehicle. If a four wheel drive is recommended or required, this is noted in the driving directions and classified as difficult.

- Easy Access and parking via a paved road.
- Moderate Access and parking via well-maintained FSR or other unpaved road. No concerns with use of a two wheel drive vehicle.
- Difficult Access via unmaintained backcountry roads. Four wheel drive may be recommended or even necessary. Pay close attention to driving directions and noted hazards.

It should be noted that our two family vehicles had minor discrepancies in their odometer readings between waypoints. This might result in slight variances in actual distance versus the information provided. As much as possible, a landmark or reference is provided with each distance to ensure access descriptions are as accurate as possible.

SAFETY ON RESOURCE ROADS

Forestry Service Roads are typically one- or two-lane gravel roads built for industrial purposes to access natural resources in remote areas. They are used primarily by vehicles engaged in forestry, mining, oil and gas or agriculture operations. In addition to industrial access, resource roads are used by the general public and commercial operators, such as backcountry skiing or hunting businesses and lodges or other accommodators. FSRs serve as crucial links for rural communities and access to recreational opportunities.

As they are not built or maintained to the same standards as public highways, resource roads can be rough with narrow gravel surfaces. There may be roadside brush limiting visibility, soft shoulders, more curves, tighter curves and much steeper grades than are encountered on public highways. These roads do not necessarily have signs or barriers identifying all hazards or dangers. Common dangers include large industrial vehicles; high traffic volume; poor visibility due to brush, alignment, dust, fog or smoke; passing or being

13

Diving, jumping, or kayaking into the pools or creek below Sutherland Falls is **extremely dangerous**. Most people are hurt.

You assume all liability for your actions should you attempt it.

BRITISH
COLUMBIA

passed on narrow roads; changing road surface conditions; weather; wildlife and so forth. A radio is recommended on resource roads that are actively being used for forestry or mining. It is also a good idea to drive with your headlights on to improve your own visibility.

Resource road users must drive with caution at all times!

Waterfall safety

Waterfalls are incredibly beautiful but can be incredibly dangerous. In the age of smart phones, social media and the selfie, more and more people are taking risks to get The Shot. Most of these safety tips should be common sense, but you know what they say about common sense!

1. Stay on established trails. Not only does deviating from trails destroy vegetation but undeveloped terrain can be highly unstable. Hiking off trail might also put others below you at risk, as soil or rocks can be knocked loose.

2. Don't swim or cross creeks above waterfalls. One wrong step and a strong current can take you from the top of a waterfall to the bottom in a split second. Some locations have designated viewing areas or fencing to restrict access to dangerous or unstable terrain. These fences, guards and railings are in place for your safety.

3. Don't. Jump. Off. Waterfalls. Period. There are so many factors to consider, including water depth, currents and rocks or debris below the surface. Pools can change from year to year, even season to season, with runoff carrying rocks, logs and debris downstream. Water levels change seasonally and can also be affected by rainfall. Never assume a pool is safe. People have died at some of the waterfalls described in this very book. Again: don't jump off waterfalls.

4. Avoid rocks and climbing at the base of waterfalls. Spray and mist make rocks and trails slippery, especially near the pools at the base of falls.

5. Watch for streamflow advisories (usually posted during spring runoff). Water can rise up over established trails or creek crossings. The higher volume in spring creates fast-moving water, debris flows and bank erosion. Streamflow can increase by as much as 15 times the normal volume, especially during periods of rapid melting and high runoff.

6. Wear appropriate footwear. A good pair of light hikers is a must for most hikes. Trails may be slippery, especially as you approach waterfalls. If you need to cross a creek, best to have a pair of water shoes or a full-coverage sandal that can be secured to your foot at the top and back (read: flip-flops are not appropriate footwear).

Hiking with kids

One of the biggest hurdles we faced as new parents was to find a variety of short, easy hikes to take our kids on. Most of the hiking guides currently in print describe breathtaking vistas, shimmering mountain lakes and, without a doubt, some of the highest-value scenery in the world. Many are lengthy day hikes. Some involve backcountry camping. Most include substantial elevation gain. Like many parents we transitioned from baby wraps to kid carriers to holding hands or to simply carrying kids in our arms. Some days were hugely successful, others nothing short of torturous. The one thing we craved was to have more options to transition our kids from our backs to the trails.

As a father of two I can say my biggest fault was expecting too much from my kids at too young of an age. Fortunately, I did not completely break them. So, having learned the lesson myself, the most important wisdom I can pass along is this: be patient. When patience fails, however, here are a few tips to keep kids keen on hiking.

1. Make sure they're comfortable. It might mean bringing an extra jacket, pants, toques, mitts, socks, hats and undies. If a child isn't comfortable, don't expect them to hike with you.
2. Arm yourself with games to play such as I Spy, 20 Questions, riddles or just plain old silly facts and useless information. If a child isn't interested, don't expect them to hike with you.
3. Bring snacks and take breaks. Yes, I agree that being asked to take a break five minutes from the car is annoying, and I'll leave it up to you to decide how reasonable the stop-for-a-snack request is. But if a child is hungry, don't expect them to hike with you.
4. Pick hikes that are within your kids' ability and comfort level. While carefully pushing my own children in an effort to help them grow, I will never advocate for doing something unsafe. There is also a discernible difference between comfort and safety. If a child feels unsafe, don't expect them to hike with you.
5. Take a camera. No, not for you. For the kids. Taking photos seems

to give kids a sense of purpose and achievement. They can see the results immediately; it gives them a task and keeps their interest up. Celebrate the little victories, whether it's as simple as taking a good photo or completing an easy hike. If a child doesn't feel like they've accomplished something, don't expect them to hike to with you.

6. Bring candy.

Leave No Trace

If you're like me, finding garbage in the backcountry puts me in a bad mood. And it's not just the garbage. I despise braided trails and shortcuts on switchbacks. I shudder when I happen upon random fire rings, and cairns that have no purpose. The Leave No Trace principles are critical in preserving the outdoor experience, and it is never too early to familiarize yourself with backcountry etiquette. If you consider yourself a pro is this regard, pass your knowledge along to teach the next generation of trail stewards!

THE SEVEN PRINCIPLES OF LEAVE NO TRACE

1. Plan ahead and prepare.
2. Travel and camp on durable surfaces.
3. Dispose of waste properly.
4. Leave what you find.
5. Minimize campfire impacts.
6. Respect wildlife.
7. Be considerate of other visitors.

For more information visit leavenotrace.ca.

Wildlife

What would a guidebook be without speaking about wildlife? Let's face it, this is their backyard and we are guests, so give wildlife a wide berth. You can encounter all sorts of woodland creatures at any time and without warning, including everything from ground squirrels and deer to porcupines, rattlesnakes, foxes and bears. While the discussion on an animal such as a chipmunk is limited mostly to "don't feed the chipmunks," the pep talk on an apex predator such as a grizzly bear is a slightly different chat. It is also one that warrants precious space on paper.

BEARS

"BC" of course stands for "British Columbia." But if you are hiking here, consider it to also stand for "Bear Country." While bears generally tend to avoid people, encounters do happen. The best preparation is knowledge: knowing how to avoid an encounter and knowing what to do in case of an encounter.

Avoiding an encounter is the best idea. Take precautions such as travelling in larger groups, making lots of noise and keeping dogs on leashes. Watch for fresh markings such as scat, tracks, overturned rocks and torn up logs. If you come across a dead animal, leave the area and report the carcass to a conservation officer or park staff. Carry bear spray, keep it easily accessible and know how to use it.

If you do encounter a bear, stay calm and have your bear spray ready to use. Speak to the bear in a firm voice. Make yourself appear as large as possible and back away slowly. Stay together in your group and pick up small children. If you're carrying a backpack, leave it on. Either wait for the bear to move on, give it a wide berth or slowly back away and leave the area. Report encounters to a conservation officer or parks staff.

If the bear escalates its behaviour and charges, be prepared and use your bear spray. If the bear attacks and makes contact, play dead by lying on your stomach with your hands over the back of your neck. However, if the attack continues for more than two minutes, fight back. We recommend reading other resources on bear safety. The more knowledge you have about bear behaviour, avoiding encounters and using bear spray, the better prepared you will be in bear country. Parks Canada and WildSafeBC both have excellent information available for free.

I had my closest bear encounter on one of the trails described in this guide: Little McPhee Falls, near Castlegar. I came across two cubs ahead of me on the trail after rounding a curve. By the time I realized how close I was to the cubs, I was already between them and their mama. I located her quickly, had my bear spray on hand and backed away slowly while addressing the mother bear. Fortunately the bears moved on and I certainly didn't stick around for a photo opportunity. I then reported the encounter to the conservation office. This could have ended very badly and I am extremely thankful I had taken the time over the years to learn how to manage an encounter.

ADDITIONAL NOTES ON WILDLIFE

The primary objective when it comes to wildlife conflicts while recreating outdoors is to reduce the opportunities for encounters altogether. The best thing you can do is arm yourself with knowledge. Know what types of wildlife you can expect to come across and how to deal with a direct encounter. Be vigilant with food and garbage. Animals that are fed become habituated to human interactions and the chances of conflicts with animals become much higher.

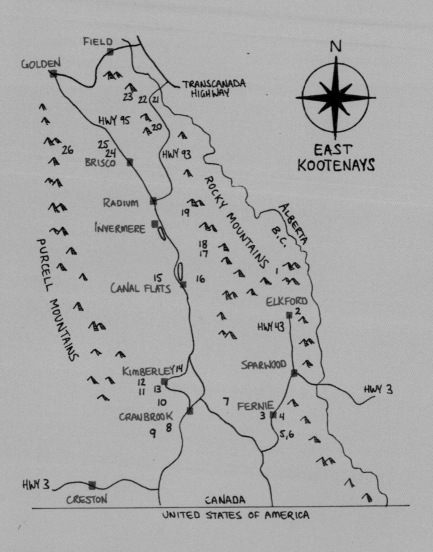

CHAPTER 1

East Kootenay

The East Kootenay region is a long north–south valley and home to the Columbia and Kootenay rivers. The region is bordered by the Rocky Mountains and the Great Divide to the east, the Trans-Canada corridor to the north, the Purcell Mountains to the west and the United States border to the south. Within this area are numerous provincial parks as well as the gem that is Kootenay National Park.

Highway 3 traverses the southern portion of the region, providing travellers both an east–west route near the US border and access to southern Alberta via the Crowsnest Pass. Highway 93/95 runs north–south and facilitates connection with the Trans-Canada Highway as well as providing access to Alberta via Banff National Park.

Cranbrook is the largest city and economic hub in the region, offering plenty of amenities for travellers. With that being said, most communities in the region have extensive services, including fuel, groceries and accommodations. Additional towns along Highway 3 providing full amenities include Elkford, Sparwood and Fernie. Towns on the Highway 93/95 corridor that offer full services include Kimberley, Canal Flats, Fairmont, Invermere and Radium.

1. Pétain Falls

LOCATION: Elk Lakes Provincial Park, Elkford
DRIVING DIFFICULTY: Moderate
HIKING DIFFICULTY: Moderate
HIKING DISTANCE: 7.2 km
HIKING TIME: 2.5–3.5 hr.

Why Elk Lakes Provincial Park is not busier is beyond my comprehension. This place has it all and most people don't even know it exists. Sure, it's a long drive down a forestry road just to get within sniffing distance of the park, but it is worth every tire-jarring bump to get there. Once you are at the trailhead, the journey is just beginning. Tucked away amongst limestone giants, alpine streams and mountain lakes is the spectacular Pétain Falls!

Driving directions

From the town of Elkford, head north on the Elk River FSR, following BC Parks signage for Elk Lakes Provincial Park. Just north of town the road transitions to gravel but is well maintained for the first 40 km. The last 30 km of road to the trailhead narrows and becomes fairly rough. Allow 90 minutes from Elkford to the parking area and signed trailhead.

Hiking directions

From the trailhead, follow a well-maintained and well-marked trail signed for Upper Elk Lake and Pétain Falls. You will pass the Elk Lakes Cabin (operated by the Alpine Club of Canada) followed by Lower Elk Lake and the main campground. After reaching the Upper Lake, the trail becomes a little more rugged along the lakeshore. As you leave the shoreline and enter the outwash area at the end of the lake, flagging and cairns mark the route through the gravel flats before the trail re-enters the forest. Continue following trail markers signed for Pétain Falls.

The route to Pétain is a long day out, especially if you aren't staying overnight at the cabin or the main campground. However, it is a beautiful hike, gains very little elevation along the way and is well worth the effort.

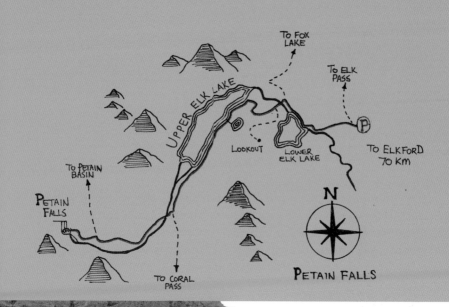

Know before you go

The flood event of 2013 washed out parts of the trail past the Upper Lake as well as the original Pétain Creek campground. Wilderness camping is still permitted at the site, where a couple of tent pads were cleared of rocks and debris left over from the flood. There is a cooking area, bear locker and outhouse. The campground is not marked on the trail anymore nor is it referenced on the current provincial park map, but it is a beautiful and quiet spot only 1.5 km from the end of the Upper Lake and 1.5 km to Pétain Falls. The trail sits across from the outhouse and descends into a rocky flat.

2. Josephine Falls

LOCATION: Elkford
DRIVING DIFFICULTY: Easy
HIKING DIFFICULTY: Easy
HIKING DISTANCE: 2.5 km
HIKING TIME: 45 min.

Known more for coal mining than for hiking, the village of Elkford will surprise you with its easy access to many trails and wilderness opportunities. Josephine Falls isn't exactly wilderness, but it is a good opportunity to break yourself in slowly while exploring the trails around this small mining town.

Driving directions

From the main intersection (four-way stop) in the town of Elkford, turn east onto the Fording River Road. Reset your trip odometer. Follow the paved Fording River Road for 4.8 km to an unmarked parking area on the right for Josephine Falls and for Lily and Lost lakes.

Hiking directions

From the trailhead, immediately follow the signed left fork for Josephine Falls. The trail is well-used and well-maintained but with lots of roots, so watch your step. At 2.5 km you will come to a fenced viewpoint and picnic area overlooking the falls.

Return the way you came or continue on to Lost Lake and Lily Lake to complete the loop. The trail is accessible by early May and generally snow free until late October, or bring your snowshoes and tackle it in the winter months. The falls can be viewed year-round but are most impressive in May and June during runoff. Although one of the most popular trails around Elkford, Josephine Falls is secluded and quiet.

Silly fact

The falls were reportedly discovered by Professor Henry Fairfield Osborn, who named them in honour of his daughter, Josephine Osborn. She caught the largest recorded trout from that location at the time.

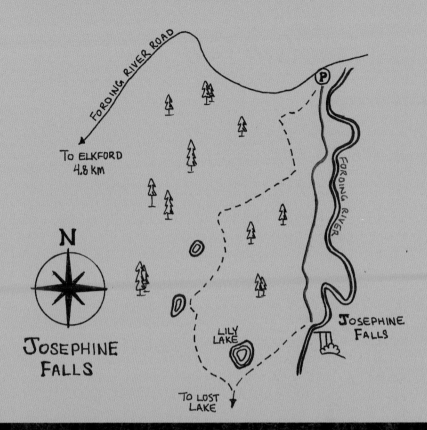

FORDING RIVER ROAD

P

TO ELKFORD
4.8 km

FORDING RIVER

N

JOSEPHINE
FALLS

LILY
LAKE

JOSEPHINE
FALLS

TO LOST
LAKE

3. Fairy Creek Falls

LOCATION: Fernie
DRIVING DIFFICULTY: Easy
HIKING DIFFICULTY: Easy
HIKING DISTANCE: 2.0 km
HIKING TIME: 40 min.

Fairy Creek Falls is one of the most popular trails near Fernie and it won't take long to figure out why. This is a classic local hike in any season and a great way to stretch your legs if you are simply passing through town. It's also a great destination in itself. The falls are accessible year-round, although snowshoes might be required in the winter months or after a heavy snowfall.

Driving directions

From downtown Fernie, head east on Highway 3. Cross the Elk River and turn in to the parking area for the Fernie Visitor Centre, highlighted by a large wooden oil derrick. Park here. Trailhead information and signage are beside the visitor centre.

Hiking directions

From the trailhead, follow a well-used and well-marked trail to the falls. Green trail markers lead the way alongside Fairy Creek to the base of the waterfall. Numerous other trails and roads intersect the main trail and are used heavily by mountain bikers. Be aware of other users, as this is one of the most popular recreation areas in Fernie in the summer.

What's with the wooden tower?

The wooden oil derrick at the trailhead is a reconstruction of the Akamina No. 2 derrick which operated near Fernie in the Flathead River Valley prior to the First World War. The original, Akamina No. 1, was the first oil well drilled in British Columbia, in 1907. When tools were lost in the hole the well was abandoned. Components were transferred to Akamina No. 2, which ended with a similar fate. Small petroleum discoveries in the late 1800s led to exploration, and a number of drilling operations near Fernie were worked from 1907 to 1930.

Petroleum extraction never took hold in the region, and with coal mining and forestry booming, oil was quickly forgotten. Today the Elk Valley remains a hub for the coal industry, although Fernie itself is more recognizable as a ski destination.[1]

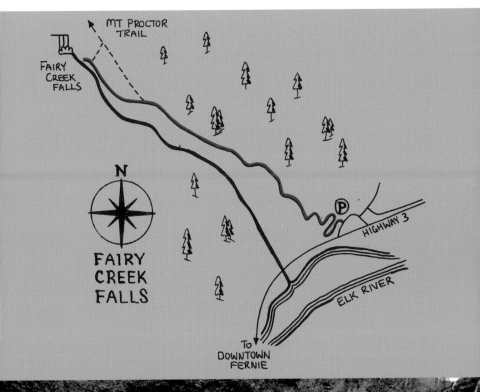

4. Matheson Falls

LOCATION: Fernie
DRIVING DIFFICULTY: Moderate
HIKING DIFFICULTY: Moderate (due to creek crossing)
HIKING DISTANCE: 1.5 km
HIKING TIME: 25 min.

If Fairy Creek Falls is one of the best-known hikes around Fernie, Matheson Falls would be the opposite. There is no trailhead kiosk here and the creek crossing may prevent you from seeing the falls altogether, but the reward for a little extra work is one of Fernie's hidden gems. Although Matheson Falls is only modest in height, what it lacks in stature it makes up for in ambience. The moss-rimmed bowl that encircles the waterfall will have you feeling much more secluded than just a 10-minute drive from town would have you believe.

Driving directions

Drive into downtown Fernie via 4th Street. At the four-way stop, continue straight through and cross the railway tracks. Turn right on Pine Ave. Pass the Aquatic Centre and turn left onto Coal Creek Road, which passes alongside homes before becoming a well-used gravel road. Reset your trip odometer. At 5.3 km stay right and cross a bridge. At 9.1 km cross a second bridge and park on the left-hand side of the road in a wide, unmarked pullout.

Hiking directions

Walk back across to the right side of the road and pick up a trail that drops off the roadside. The trail works its way along the left-hand side of the creek. After a few hundred metres the trail meets the creek and bends to the left. You can shimmy across on a downed log or find a calm, low-water spot to ford. Note that this may not be safe or even possible during runoff or periods of high stream flow. Pick up the trail again on the right-hand side of the creek and follow it to the base of the waterfall. Occasionally the trail drops down out of the forest onto rocks in the creekbed. These are generally slick, so use caution. Best time to view is midsummer to early October when the water levels are lower.

COAL CREEK

COAL CREEK ROAD

Ⓟ

N

TO FERNIE, HIGHWAY 3

MATHESON FALLS

MATHESON FALLS

5. Morrissey Falls (Upper)

LOCATION: Fernie
DRIVING DIFFICULTY: Moderate
HIKING DIFFICULTY: Moderate (due to steepness of trail)
HIKING DISTANCE: <100 m
HIKING TIME: 5 min.

Morrissey Falls may be the least-known waterfall in the Kootenays. Many people driving Morrissey Road probably have no idea of the spectacle on display beyond their driver's side window. The creek is just enough out of sight that not one but two good sized waterfalls, the Upper and Lower Morrissey Falls, are concealed from view yet only spitting distance away.

Driving directions

From Fernie drive west on Highway 3 to Morrissey Road (signed). Turn left (south) onto Morrissey Road. Reset your trip odometer. Cross the bridge over the Elk River and stay right. At 3.7 km the road

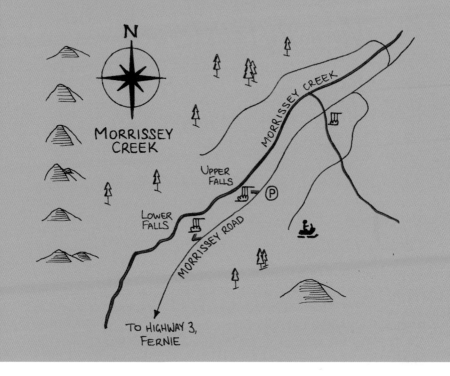

splits in three directions; stay straight. Stay left at 5.6 km. Stay left again at 7.4 km. Follow Morrissey Road to 12.2 km. The road widens slightly with a small pullout on the left. Turn around and park here.

Hiking directions

From your car Morrissey Falls can be heard below. A faint trail drops sharply off the side of the road directly to the base of the falls. The trail is *very* steep and slippery, especially if wet, so tread carefully. Morrissey Creek falls into a small bowl ringed by cliffs.

Some obscure history

At the turn of the 1900s, the Crowsnest Pass Coal Company was so adamant about Morrissey's coal-mining prospects that the Canadian Pacific Railway completed the Crowsnest Branch line by 1898. The operation turned up poor-quality coal, however, and was plagued by accidents, eventually leading to its premature closure in 1909. The site was used as an internment camp during the First World War and finally shut down in 1918. Today Morrissey is better known for its snowmobiling than its coal production.[2]

6. Morrissey Falls (Lower)

LOCATION: Fernie
DRIVING DIFFICULTY: Moderate
HIKING DIFFICULTY: Moderate (due to steepness of trail)
HIKING DISTANCE: 300 m
HIKING TIME: 10 min.

Everyone likes free things. Two for one deals are basically free things. So, when you roll up the Morrissey Road to see one waterfall, don't leave without cashing in on its equally impressive twin just below.

Driving directions

As per Morrissey Falls (Upper), drive west on Highway 3 to Morrissey Road (signed). Turn left (south) onto Morrissey Road. Reset your trip odometer. Cross the bridge over the Elk River and stay right. At 3.7 km the road splits in three directions; stay straight. Stay left at 5.6 km. Stay left again at 7.4 km. Follow Morrissey Road to 12.2 km. The road widens slightly with a small pullout on the left. Turn around and park here.

Hiking directions

From the pullout, walk back down the road about 200 m. Keep your eye on the creek and you will just see the lower waterfall from the road. Similar to the upper falls, a faint boot-beaten trail drops steeply away from the road to the base of the falls. Also similar to the upper falls, use extra caution as you descend. It is *very* steep and will be extremely slippery if wet.

Bonus waterfall

Since you've gone this far, why stop at just two waterfalls? Another 200 m past the pullout/parking area for the Upper Falls, there is a third waterfall on the right as you cross a bridge. This small stream feeds Morrissey Creek below the bridge and is worth the extra minute of driving to check out.

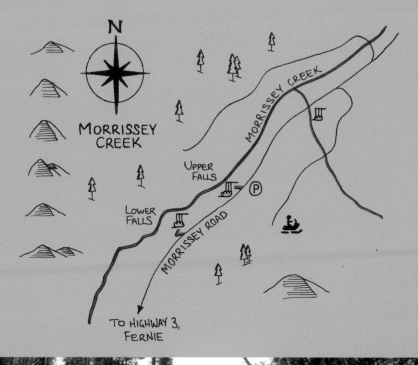

N

MORRISSEY CREEK

MORRISSEY CREEK

UPPER FALLS

Ⓟ

LOWER FALLS

MORRISSEY ROAD

TO HIGHWAY 3, FERNIE

7. Cliff Lake Falls

LOCATION: Cranbrook
DRIVING DIFFICULTY: Difficult (4WD required)
HIKING DIFFICULTY: Easy (to view of falls)
HIKING DISTANCE: 1.5 km
HIKING TIME: 40 min.

Do you hate your car? You can prove it by forcing it up the Van Creek forestry service road to the Cliff Lake trail. Or, better yet, grab a buddy's truck to check out Cliff Lake Falls. The waterfall itself is a vertical stream cartwheeling down the headwall below Cliff Lake with a total elevation drop that is quite impressive. If you have made the effort to get a view of the falls, don't stop there. While the route to Cliff Lake is a bit of a grunt, the view up top is worth every step.

Driving directions

From Cranbrook, drive south on Highway 3/93. Cross the Kootenay River bridge at Wardner and turn left onto the Wardner–Ft. Steele Road. Turn right onto the Bull River Road and reset your trip odometer. At 8.1 km cross the bridge over the canyon (worth stopping for a look into the gorge from the bridge). At 8.3 km make a left-hand turn (note: you will still be on the Bull River Road). Drive to 19.7 km and turn left onto the signed Van Creek Road. Cross a creek at 28.6 km and look for a pullout on the left with a signed trailhead for the Cliff Lake Trail (at the 41 km sign).

Note: The Van Creek road deteriorates rapidly, with rocky washouts at 20.2 km and 22.7 km. A high-clearance SUV or truck is required for negotiating these washouts.

Hiking directions

From the signed trailhead, follow a moderately used but well-maintained trail. There are numerous trails that break away from the main trail, but they usually end quickly or reconnect with the main path. At around 1.5 km the trail meets the creek and a steep, slabby rock face. Scramble up the rock where the view of Cliff Lake Falls opens up shortly thereafter. Travel to Cliff Lake beyond this point is via a faint, boot-beaten trail marked by cairns which gains steep elevation up the headwall on the right side of the creek and waterfalls.

More to explore

Beyond Cliff Lake Falls and Cliff Lake there is a paradise to explore. A series of high alpine passes moves you from basin to basin, tarn to tarn, and gets you within range of one of the most southerly glaciers in Canada. For trail descriptions, check out *Mountain Footsteps* by Cranbrook author Janice Strong.

8. Moyie Falls (Lumberton Falls)

LOCATION: Cranbrook, BC
DRIVING DIFFICULTY: Moderate
HIKING DIFFICULTY: Easy (see hiking directions)
HIKING DISTANCE: 1.0 km
HIKING TIME: 25 min.

Some call it Moyie Falls, some call it Lumberton Falls. Regardless of the title, this waterfall is a beauty and is fast becoming one of Cranbrook's most poorly kept secrets. Expect to get your feet wet... a small price to pay for admission to enjoy a place like this so close to town.

Driving directions

From Cranbrook, drive west on Highway 3 to Lumberton Road. Turn right (west) onto Lumberton Road. Reset your trip odometer. Drive 7.2 km on a well-used and well-maintained gravel road. At 7.2 km the road bends sharply to the right and there is a small spur road on the left. Either park at the bend in the road or drive 100 m down the spur road to a turnaround that has lots of space for parking.

Hiking directions

At the turnaround, head for the yellow gate, which is locked due to former mining and logging operations in the vicinity. The road, approach and falls, however, are on public, Crown land. Walk past the gate and down the road to the river. The simplest approach is to wade across the river (mid-shin depth by late summer) and then continue along the road on the opposite side to get near the base of the falls. Alternatively, once you're at the bottom of the hill, continue through a grassy area and down into the riverbed. Follow the riverbed until the falls are in view (easy to this point in low water).

Accessing the base of the falls is a little trickier. From the end of the road, scramble up and over a steep, muddy slope to the large rocks at the base of the falls. If you have hiked in via the riverbed, a steep, narrow trail on the right bank skirts the river to the base of the falls. Tread carefully, as the rocks in the riverbed are rounded and usually wet, making them quite slippery. While the falls are accessible year-round, crossing the river is not recommended during runoff or

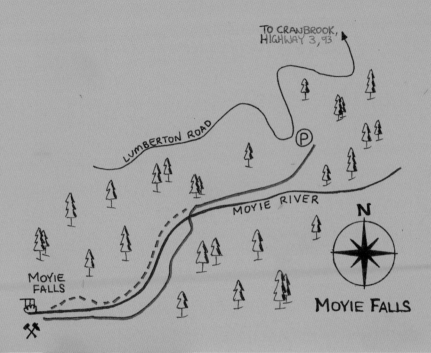

MOYIE FALLS

periods of high stream flow. Sturdy sandals for the crossing are advised.

Random local history

Moyie Falls is home to the "Lucky Friday Minesite," an old gold mining claim now extending nearly 250 m underground near the falls. The underground channel was originally discovered in 1894. Remnants of nearly 125 years of mining are scattered around the site, including the two main entrances. There is an active placer claim in the area and the site is occasionally worked by the claim holders.[3]

9. Lewisby Falls (unofficial name)

LOCATION: Cranbrook
DRIVING DIFFICULTY: Moderate
HIKING DIFFICULTY: Easy
HIKING DISTANCE: 300 m
HIKING TIME: 10 min.

Never heard of Lewisby Falls? You're not alone. In fact, we're not sure it has a name let alone if Lewisby is correct. It's also not much of a waterfall; however, if summer swimming holes are your thing, this one is not too shabby (albeit a little brisk).

Driving directions

From Cranbrook: head west on Highway 3/93. Turn right onto Lumberton Road about 10 km west of town. Reset your trip odometer. There are numerous branch roads that intersect the main Lumberton Forestry Service Road. Stay left at 8.6 km. Stay right at 12.2 km. Take a left at 18.1 km onto the Ridgeway Main Forestry Service Road. Cross a bridge at 20.0 km and turn right immediately after the bridge. After a hundred metres there is a small clearing and an old picnic area where you can park.

Hiking directions

Continue on the dirt road for about 250 m. Pass a cabin on the left which is owned and operated by the Cranbrook Snowmobile Club (please respect their cabin and grounds). Shortly after the cabin, there is a trail on the right that leaves the road. Follow that to the creek and down into the creekbed. Once in the creekbed, backtrack downstream a short distance to get a better view of the small waterfall. During periods of high water and runoff, the creek drops over a small rocky outcrop to a great little swimming hole. As the water levels fall throughout the summer, the creek bypasses the feature that creates the waterfall. Best viewed in May and June during runoff or drop by later in the summer for a swim.

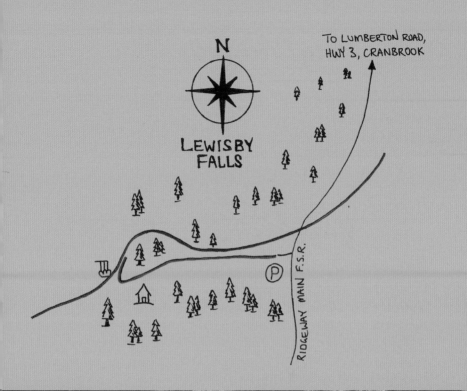

N

LEWISBY
FALLS

TO LUMBERTON ROAD,
HWY 3, CRANBROOK

RIDGEWAY MAIN F.S.R.

10. Perry Creek Falls

LOCATION: Cranbrook
DRIVING DIFFICULTY: Moderate
HIKING DIFFICULTY: Easy
HIKING DISTANCE: 1.5 km
HIKING TIME: 30 min.

Perry Creek Falls is a classic short day hike and local favourite in the East Kootenays. A mellow trail leads to a stunning multi-tiered waterfall tucked into a narrow canyon.

Driving directions

From Cranbrook, drive north on Highway 95A to Wycliffe Park Road and turn left. Reset your trip odometer. Drive 1.9 km to Wycliffe Road and turn right. At 2.7 km turn right onto the Perry Creek road. At 6.4 km stay left on the primary road. At 8.4 km stay right and cross the bridge over Perry Creek. At 13.0 km look for a small dirt road on the left and pull into the parking area.

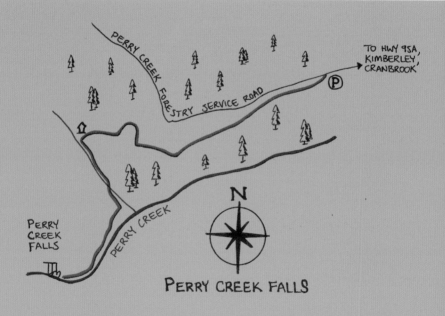

PERRY CREEK FALLS

Hiking directions

From the car park, walk through an old brown gate and follow the road for about 10 minutes. The road will bend down to the left and end in a small grassy clearing. Pick up a well-used trail at the end of the clearing and descend to the left after passing an old cabin. The trail follows the left side of a small stream before coming to an old, rotting footbridge, which is used to make the crossing.

After crossing the bridge and a brief descent, the trail splits. Stay right. The trail descends slightly and follows the right-hand side of Perry Creek. A couple of narrow and slippery sections require careful footing before you reach the falls shortly after.

Back in the day...

Perry Creek was another area utilized for gold mining in the same era as the Wildhorse Gold Rush, but without the same fanfare. Although the waterwheel and steam shovel used in mining operations have been relocated and reconstructed at the historic Fort Steele Heritage Town near Cranbrook, there are still lots of signs of the age-old industry scattered throughout the Perry Creek valley.

11. Marysville Falls

LOCATION: Kimberley
DRIVING DIFFICULTY: Easy
HIKING DIFFICULTY: Easy
HIKING DISTANCE: 300 m
HIKING TIME: 5 min.

Standing at the overlook at Marysville Falls, it is easy to forget you are mere minutes from town, and on foot no less. Just a few hundred metres from the main highway through Marysville in south Kimberley is a serene pathway that leads to one of the highlights of the area. When you're done this lovely and short stroll, head up to Kimberley's downtown plaza (a pedestrian mall called the Platzl) and check out the many shops and restaurants, or drive the St. Mary Lake road up the valley and take advantage of some of the recreation opportunities there.

Driving directions

From downtown Kimberley, drive south towards Marysville on Highway 95A (about five minutes). As you enter Marysville, a bridge crosses Mark Creek. You can pull over to the curb on the right side of the road or make a quick left into a signed parking area.

Hiking directions

The signed trailhead on the south side of the highway marks the start of the short hike to a very impressive waterfall right in town. Cross the creek using the large, timber-frame bridge and follow boardwalks and a broad path along the creek to a fenced lookout. The falls are well worth checking out at any time of the year, as they are deafening with springtime runoff and often fully frozen in winter.

For your information

The Marysville Falls trail was originally planned and designed by the Kimberley Rotary Club in 1978. The route was formally opened in 1982 after four years of volunteer efforts to construct the original bridge, boardwalks and trail to, and viewpoint at, the 30-metre waterfall.

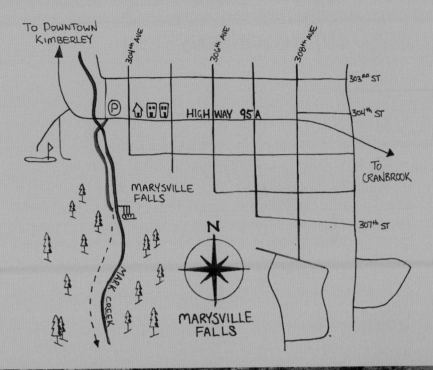

To DOWNTOWN KIMBERLEY

304ᵗʰ AVE   306ᵗʰ AVE   308ᵗʰ AVE

303ᴿᴰ ST

HIGHWAY 95 A

304ᵗʰ ST

TO CRANBROOK

MARYSVILLE FALLS

307ᵗʰ ST

N

MARK CREEK

MARYSVILLE FALLS

12. Meachen Falls

LOCATION: Kimberley
DRIVING DIFFICULTY: Moderate
HIKING DIFFICULTY: Easy
HIKING DISTANCE: 200 m
HIKING TIME: 5 min.

If you are visiting Kimberley and ask anyone in town what to see or do, they are probably going to answer with "Meachen Falls!" without a second thought. While the road in is a little rough, it is a quick tromp to a big, thundering waterfall, one where you can easily get spectacular views from both above and across from the falls. This thing is deafening in late spring or early summer when runoff is at its peak, and it flows with intensity late into summer and early autumn.

Driving directions

From downtown Kimberley, drive south on Highway 95A to St. Mary Lake Road and turn right (signed). Drive west on St. Mary Lake Road for 16 km and turn left at a large signed intersection for Lakeside Road. Reset your trip odometer. Cross the bridge over the St. Mary River and turn right onto Hellroaring Creek Forestry Service Road at 0.6 km. Turn right at 1.6 km onto the Meachen Creek Forestry Service Road. Follow the Meachen Creek FSR to 9.6 km and park on the right-hand side of a large widening in the road.

Hiking directions

From the car park, a well-used trail enters the trees on the right. Shortly after entering the trees the trail splits to both left and right. The left-hand route goes to the top of the falls. Exercise extreme caution on the rocks here, as they are quite smooth and can be extremely slippery when wet. The right-hand trail travels for a couple minutes to a large rocky outcrop that makes a great viewpoint of the impressive falls. Meachen Falls is accessible from late May to late October and is impressive any time of year.

It is possible to get to the base of the falls by descending a steep trail behind the rocky overlook and down to Meachen Creek, and then following the creek back around to the base of the falls. The faint,

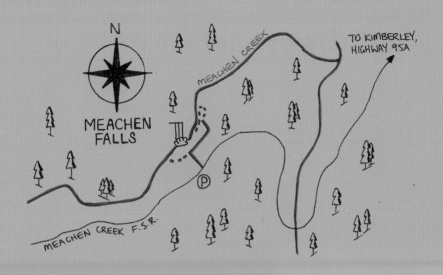

boot-beaten trail is quite steep and often damp, making it very slippery. Use extreme caution and remember: what goes down has to come back up!

13. Mary Anne Falls

LOCATION: Kimberley
DRIVING DIFFICULTY: Easy
HIKING DIFFICULTY: Moderate (see description)
HIKING DISTANCE: 1.6 km
HIKING TIME: 1 hr.

Unlike Meachen Falls just across the lake, if you are picking the brains of locals for hiking options you probably won't hear mention of this waterfall. It is tucked partway up Bootleg Mountain and hidden from view from any angle. The trail is fairly steep and at times indistinct, but the falls themselves are quite impressive. Due to the south-facing aspect of the approach, the trail to the falls is generally accessible by late April and stays clear well in to November most years.

Driving directions

From downtown Kimberley, drive south on Highway 95A towards Marysville. Between Kimberley and Marysville, turn right onto the signed St. Mary Lake Road. Reset your trip odometer here. Drive about 800 m past the end of the paved road. Park at the 17.6 km mark on the lake side of the gravel road, at a small widening of the shoulder.

Hiking directions

Cross the road from where you parked and look for an opening in the trees, sometimes flagged. Pick up a boot-beaten trail and begin the hike up. After about 20 minutes a trail forks to the right. Ignore this. Another 10 minutes later the trail splits again. You can either stay left through the bushes (recommended) or you can head to the right and follow cairns across a talus rock slope.

After about 45 minutes of hiking, you'll come to a small creekbed which is usually dry. You will hear the water running under the rocks or there may be water running in this creek during seasons with unusually high runoff. After crossing the creekbed, the trail begins a short, steep climb up a loose, rubbly slope to a rocky perch overlooking the waterfall.

The trail has been given a moderate rating because it can be indistinct and tough to follow at times. Flagging tape and cairns generally

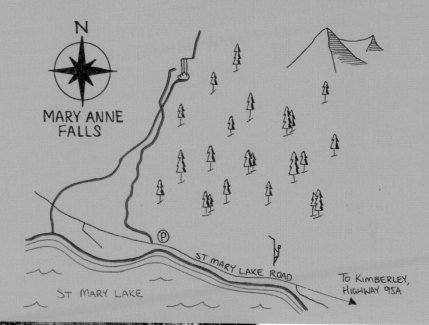

mark the way. The route to Mary Anne Falls also gains significant elevation in a relatively short hike: nearly 380 m to the overlook. The best time of year to view the falls is during spring runoff, as melting snow from Bootleg Mountain feeds this waterfall.

Remember to check all members of your party, including pets, for ticks if hiking from April to June.

14. Cherry Creek Falls

LOCATION: Kimberley
DRIVING DIFFICULTY: Moderate
HIKING DIFFICULTY: Easy
HIKING DISTANCE: 300 m
HIKING TIME: 5 min.

Driving directions

From Kimberley, drive north on Highway 95A to Thomason Road and turn left, following signs for Cherry Creek Falls Regional Park. Reset your trip odometer. Drive 0.4 km to Clarricoates Road and turn right. At 1.4 km the paved road ends. Continue to 2.1 km and turn right, into a parking area just past the bridge (signed).

Hiking directions

Follow the large maintained pathway from the car park down to the wooden stairs and guardrails. The falls are easily viewed from the bottom or the top of the stairs. There are picnic benches and firepits, making Cherry Creek a great quiet place to spend an afternoon for a barbecue or a short walk around if you are hanging out in Kimberley. The falls are accessible year-round, although the stairs to the creek are generally closed in winter for safety reasons.

For your information

In 2011 an application was submitted by private interests to establish a quarry on a site adjacent to the falls. Local residents and government rallied against the application and the mineral tenure holder forfeited the claim, paving the way for the community association to purchase the land and establish the area as a park in 2013. Cherry Creek Falls Regional Park is an excellent example of how even small-scale citizen engagement can be effective in protecting land.

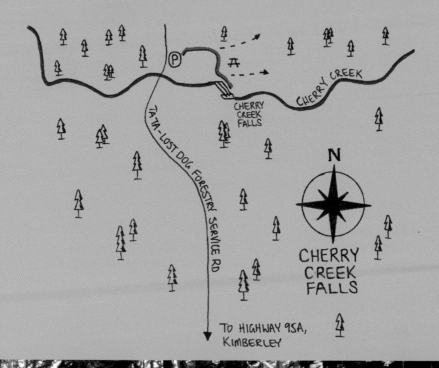

CHERRY CREEK

CHERRY
CREEK
FALLS

TA-TA-LOST DOG FORESTRY SERVICE RD

N

CHERRY
CREEK
FALLS

TO HIGHWAY 95A,
KIMBERLEY

15. Findlay Falls

LOCATION: Canal Flats
DRIVING DIFFICULTY: Moderate
HIKING DIFFICULTY: Easy
HIKING DISTANCE: 500 m
HIKING TIME: 15 min.

Driving directions

From Canal Flats, drive north on Highway 93/95 to Findlay Creek Forestry Service Road (signed) and turn left. Reset your trip odometer. Follow the Findlay Creek road for 4.7 km. Turn left into a large clearing and park at the signed trailhead.

Hiking directions

At the west end of the parking area, a brown pole signifies the trailhead. Follow the well-used trail down through thin trees for about 400 m, ignoring trails that branch off to the left. Just before the creek, the trail cuts across a steep eroded section held in place by a fallen tree. Take care crossing this short section and then drop down to a small rocky shore at the edge of the creek.

Findlay Falls is tucked in between a couple of large boulders which obscure the small cascade when the water is low. The falls are much more impressive during spring runoff or periods of high stream flow. They are also typically accessible for a short stroll in the winter months, depending on snowfall.

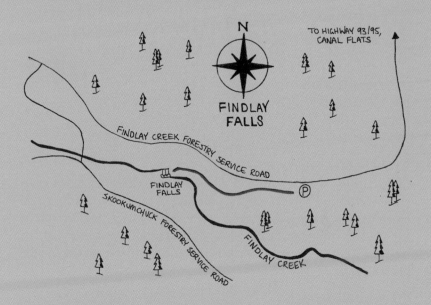

N

FINDLAY
FALLS

TO HIGHWAY 93/95,
CANAL FLATS

FINDLAY CREEK FORESTRY SERVICE ROAD

FINDLAY
FALLS

Ⓟ

SKOOKUMCHUCK FORESTRY SERVICE ROAD

FINDLAY CREEK

16. Gibraltar Wall

LOCATION: Canal Flats
DRIVING DIFFICULTY: Moderate
HIKING DIFFICULTY: Easy
HIKING DISTANCE: 300 m
HIKING TIME: 10 min.

In the spring, summer and fall, Gibraltar Wall is nothing more than a wet smear on a cliff face. But by the end of December during an average winter, the smear freezes, forming a massive fortification of ice nearly 100 m high. It is a popular destination for ice climbers in the East Kootenay due to its close proximity to towns in the Columbia Valley.

Driving directions

From the four-way stop at Grainger Avenue and Burns Avenue in Canal Flats, turn onto the gravel Kootenay River Forestry Service Road. Reset your trip odometer. Drive 26 km to a small pullout on your right. The frozen waterfall is visible above you. The gravel road is well-used and well-maintained although it can become quite slippery with compact snow and ice during the winter.

Hiking directions

From where you've parked your vehicle on the right-hand side of the road, cross the road and pick up a boot-beaten path through the trees. After only a few minutes, with the path weaving in and out of the trees, you'll come to an open slope below the waterfall. Take care in winter, as water from the ice wall seeps and freezes on this slope making it very slippery. The best time to see the frozen waterfall is between late December and early March.

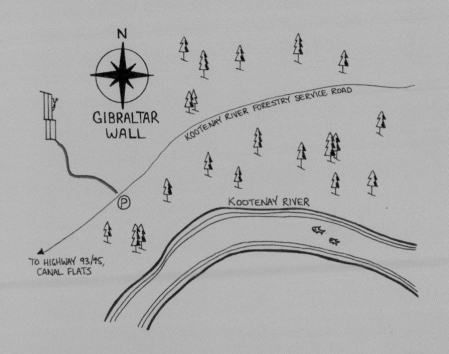

N

GIBRALTAR
WALL

KOOTENAY RIVER FORESTRY SERVICE ROAD

P

KOOTENAY RIVER

TO HIGHWAY 93/95,
CANAL FLATS

17. Pedley Falls

LOCATION: Canal Flats
DRIVING DIFFICULTY: Moderate
HIKING DIFFICULTY: Easy (see hiking directions)
HIKING DISTANCE: 1.7 km
HIKING TIME: 40 min.

If you are searching for data on Pedley Falls, well, good luck. There is no trail, no trailhead and no information for accessing or viewing the falls. In fact, the vast majority of people who have actually seen the falls first-hand have done so while rafting or paddling the Kootenay River.

Driving directions

From downtown Canal Flats, turn onto the Kootenay River Forest Service Road at the main intersection (a four-way stop) and reset your trip odometer. Follow the well-used, well-maintained gravel road. Stay to the right at 31.9 km. Cross the Kootenay River on a bridge at 32.5 km. Stay left at 33.2 km and drive to 42.2 km, where an unmaintained dirt road signed BR.A is on your left. Park here or drive down the dirt road to its end.

Hiking directions

Follow the dirt road down and around to the left, followed by a hard right-hand bend near the 1 km mark. The dirt road ends in a small clearing just beyond. From here, pick up a game trail trending south along a treed plateau above the Kootenay River. After a few hundred metres the game trail peters out in a small clearing. Bend to the right (west) back towards the river. The falls can be heard at this point, and within a few hundred metres there is an excellent overlook where Pedley Falls tumbles into the Kootenay River.

Know before you go

There is no formal trail to Pedley Falls. It could be one of the least-known waterfalls in the East Kootenay and is generally seen only from the Kootenay River itself. While several raft guiding companies in the Columbia Valley offer trips on the mighty Kootenay, if you

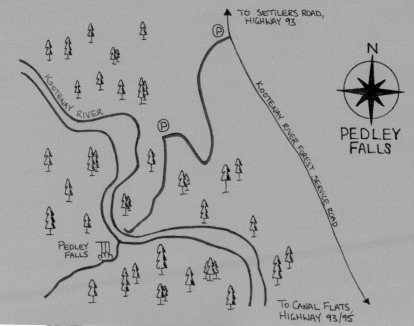

TO SETTLERS ROAD, HIGHWAY 93

KOOTENAY RIVER

KOOTENAY RIVER FOREST SERVICE ROAD

PEDLEY FALLS

N

PEDLEY FALLS

TO CANAL FLATS, HIGHWAY 93/95

do decide to hike rather than raft to the falls, this is a great little test of navigational skills without the benefit of a signed or a marked trail. Refer to the map for the rough location of the game trail where you leave the dirt road. Enjoy!

18. Fenwick Falls

LOCATION: Canal Flats
DRIVING DIFFICULTY: Moderate
HIKING DIFFICULTY: Easy
HIKING DISTANCE: 200 m
HIKING TIME: 5 min.

Hidden just out of view from the Kootenay River Road is a gorgeous waterfall rimmed by a bowl of cliffs. It is a long drive on a gravel road to get to Fenwick Falls but the rewards are plentiful, with a free campsite and easy access to the creek and waterfall, as well as access to the Kootenay River for its many paddling and fishing opportunities.

Driving directions

From Canal Flats, turn onto the Kootenay River Forestry Service Road at the main intersection (a four-way stop) and reset your trip odometer. Follow a well-used, well-maintained gravel road. Stay to the right at 31.9 km. Cross the Kootenay River on a bridge at 32.5 km. Stay left at 33.2 km. Drive to 43.4 km, where a bridge crosses Fenwick

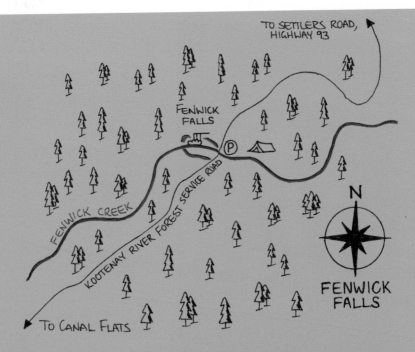

Creek. You can park in a pullout on the left-hand side of the road before the bridge or cross the bridge and pull into the recreation site on the right side of the road.

Hiking directions

Downstream of the bridge there are trails on both sides of the creek, each being only a few hundred metres in length. The first is a well-worn track that leaves the pullout before the bridge and leads to a large, flat rock right on top of the waterfall, as well as a viewing area with a wooden guardrail just beyond.

The second trail starts on the other side of the creek, across from the entry to the recreation site. It is boot beaten and cuts across steeper, slippery slopes before reaching a couple of great vantage points for the waterfall. The falls are accessible from late May to late October, but the best time to view is in June during runoff.

Know before you go

The Fenwick Creek Recreation Site offers remote, quiet, free camping and is maintained by Recreation Sites and Trails BC. There are four campsites available on a first-come, first-served basis and it is popular in the fall with hunters. Forestry recreation sites are a privilege in British Columbia and there are many similar to Fenwick Creek. Most are user-maintained, so please do your part in keeping these areas clean for the enjoyment of others. Pack out all your garbage and leave the area as good as or better than you found it!

19. *Cross River Falls*

LOCATION: Nipika Resort
DRIVING DIFFICULTY: Moderate
HIKING DIFFICULTY: Easy
HIKING DISTANCE: 3.5 km
HIKING TIME: 1.5 hr.

The bright blue waters of the Cross River tumble down a series of small steps as they make their way towards the Kootenay River from high up in the Rocky Mountains. Nipika Resort has capitalized on the abundance of natural beauty near the confluence of the two rivers to create an outdoor recreation playground. The trail to Cross River Falls is only one of many to explore!

Driving directions

From Radium, drive east on Highway 93 into Kootenay National Park. Turn right onto Settlers Road (signed). Follow a good gravel road for 14 km to Nipika Resort. Turn left into Nipika and the hikers parking area.

Hiking directions

From the parking area there are numerous combinations of trails that lead to Cross River Falls. The most direct route is "Main Street" to "Natural Bridge Direct" to "Spin Doctor" to "Lower Bridge Trail" to "Waterfall Trail." Trail information is available at the trailhead kiosk and through Nipika Resort. The Nipika trail network is also available on Trailforks.com.

More to explore

Nipika Resort maintains over 50 km of trails in the area. Summer sees them used for hiking, biking or trail running, while in the winter they are groomed for Nordic skiing, fat biking and snowshoeing. Winter users will pay a small fee to access the trails, while admission is by donation in the summer months. Another must-see on the Nipika trail network is the Natural Bridge. For more information visit nipika.com.

PHOTO: JOHN MARRIOTT

20. Numa Falls

LOCATION: Kootenay National Park
DRIVING DIFFICULTY: Easy
HIKING DIFFICULTY: Easy
HIKING DISTANCE: 100 m
HIKING TIME: 5 min.

Numa Falls is a popular rest stop and picnic area in Kootenay National Park along Highway 93. It also serves as a trailhead and access point to the renowned Rockwall Trail high above the roadway. Here the bright blue waters of the Vermilion River contract and fall through a short, narrow canyon.

Driving directions

From the four-way stop in Radium, at the junction of Highways 93 and 95, drive east on 93 into Kootenay National Park. Follow the highway for 79.8 km and look for a signed parking area for Numa Falls on the left (west) side of the road.

Hiking directions

From the parking area follow trailhead signage to a bridge over the Vermilion River and Numa Falls, just a hundred metres away.

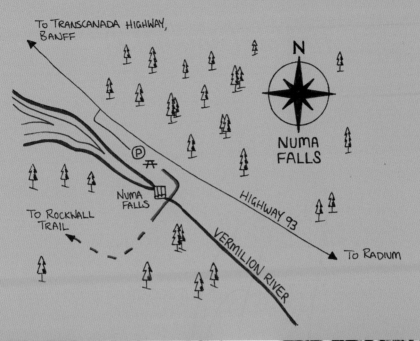

To Transcanada Highway, Banff

N

NUMA FALLS

NUMA FALLS

To Rocknall Trail

Highway 93

Vermilion River

To Radium

21. Haffner Canyon (Ice)

LOCATION: Kootenay National Park
DRIVING DIFFICULTY: Easy
HIKING DIFFICULTY: Easy (winter only)
HIKING DISTANCE: 1 km
HIKING TIME: 20 min.

Haffner is one of the more popular training grounds for ice and mixed (rock and ice) climbing, partly because it is safe in the winter, with virtually no avalanche hazard. Ice climbs typically form from water seeping through and over the rock and then freezing in layers. The canyon is relatively inaccessible in the summertime, but in winter it is transformed into a wonderland of snow and ice. The Canadian Rockies' steep limestone walls that rise up from the valley floors are home to an abundance of world-class ice climbing.

Driving directions

From Radium, drive east on Highway 93 into Kootenay National Park. It is 86.6 km from the four-way stop in Radium to the parking area. Just after you cross Haffner Creek there is an unmarked pullout on the right-hand side that ice climbers use for parking. The signed parking for Marble Canyon is a few hundred metres farther on the left, so if you end up there, you've gone just a bit too far.

Hiking directions

From the car park, follow an unmarked trail that rises into the trees on the left side of Haffner Creek. It is generally well-worn and well-used in the winter by people venturing into the canyon to climb frozen pillars of ice. The narrow canyon is inaccessible in the spring, summer and autumn because the snow and ice that cover Haffner Creek are required to access the area. Haffner is best explored from late December to mid-March.

The ice climbers trail starts in the trees and follows the left bank of the creek. After just a few minutes the trail drops down into the rocky creekbed. After about 15 minutes the trail approaches the mouth of the canyon and crosses to the right-hand side of the creek. The first few ice formations start to come into sight between the canyon walls.

Once in the canyon you can watch climbers test their skill on more than two dozen routes. If people are climbing, be sure to stay well back from the walls, as ice and rock can become dislodged. The ice formations are different every year depending on autumn and winter precipitation and temperatures. Take care crossing the creek, especially early in the season or as spring approaches.

22. Marble Canyon

LOCATION: Kootenay National Park
DRIVING DIFFICULTY: Easy
HIKING DIFFICULTY: Easy
HIKING DISTANCE: 800 m
HIKING TIME: 20 min.

Marble Canyon is one of the highlights of Kootenay National Park, if not the entire Canadian Rockies. It is a popular stop along Highway 93 at any time of the year and deservedly so. The blue waters of Tokumm Creek are squeezed through a deep, dark, narrow canyon before joining the Vermilion River near the highway. If you are stopping in a national park, you are required to hold a valid park pass, which can be purchased at the visitor centre or the park gate in Radium.

Driving directions

From the four-way stop in Radium at the junction of Highways 93 and 95, drive east on 93 to Kootenay National Park. Follow the highway for 86.8 km and look for a signed parking area for Marble Canyon on the left.

Hiking directions

From the parking area, follow the signed trail for Marble Canyon. The trail loses elevation briefly and crosses Tokumm Creek, then climbs above the canyon walls. The trail crosses the creek once again and you can walk on either side of the canyon en route to where the creek initially plunges into the chasm, creating the waterfall. Numerous bridges span the canyon, offering glimpses into the dark abyss below.

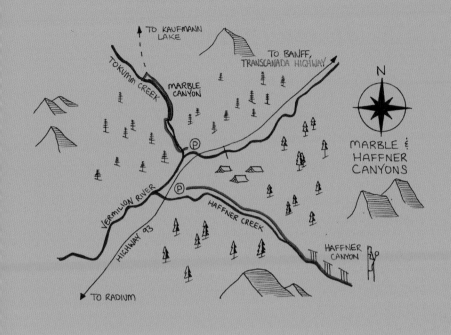

More to explore

The Tokumm Creek/Prospector's Valley trail beyond Marble Canyon is no longer maintained by Parks Canada. After the Fay Hut was lost in a fire, the route fell out of favour with backcountry enthusiasts, although it is still possible to reach Kaufmann Lake. The trail is now riddled with deadfall, but with the forest more or less scorched, the views are a little more open.

PHOTO: TOMAS NEVESELY, DREAMSTIME.COM

23. Helmet Falls

LOCATION: Kootenay National Park
DRIVING DIFFICULTY: Easy
HIKING DIFFICULTY: Difficult (due only to distance; overnight recommended)
HIKING DISTANCE: 15 km
HIKING TIME: 4–6 hrs.

At a staggering 352 vertical metres, Helmet Falls is one of the tallest waterfalls in the country, plummeting over the headwall and draining the Washmawapta Glacier. The nearby Helmet Falls campground is typically used by those hiking the Rockwall Trail, one of the premier backpacking trips in Canada. Most parties will take a relaxed five days to complete the 55 km trip while taking in the high alpine passes, meadows, lakes and 360-degree views of the lofty peaks of Kootenay National Park.

Driving directions

From Radium, drive east on Highway 93 to Kootenay National Park. Look for the signed parking area for the Paint Pots, 84 km from the four-way stop In Radium. National park and trail information, as well as outhouse facilities, are located at the busy trailhead.

Hiking directions

From the car park, follow the signed trail which crosses the Vermilion River shortly after departing. The trail is initially busy and well used by tourists scoping out the Paint Pots. After you've left the hordes behind, the trail narrows and gains elevation gently as it winds along Helmet Creek through fir, pine and spruce forests. There isn't much in terms of views along the way, but your efforts are rewarded with an incredible scene upon reaching the Helmet Creek warden's cabin 14 km later.

From the cabin, cross the creek and pass through the campground. It is recommended to spend a night here before either returning the way you came or continuing along the spectacular Rockwall Trail. A few hundred metres past the campground, the main trail bends to the left and a lesser used trail continues straight ahead to the base of the waterfall. The extra kilometre is well worth the effort to stand

under one of the country's tallest cascades. The hike is recommended for mid-July to the end of September and would be considered inaccessible in the winter months.

Know before you go

Reservations at the Helmet Falls campground are required and can be made online through Parks Canada at reservation.pc.gc.ca or by calling 1-877-RESERVE (1-877-737-3783).

24. Brisco Falls

LOCATION: Brisco
DRIVING DIFFICULTY: Moderate
HIKING DIFFICULTY: Easy
HIKING DISTANCE: 250 m
HIKING TIME: 5 min.

Brisco Falls is a hidden gem and a short trip that is tucked out of sight from the roadway. It is often bypassed by hikers and climbers hell-bent on reaching the Bugaboos... if only they knew about this secluded oasis mere minutes from the road.

Driving directions

From Radium, drive north on Highway 95 for about 20 minutes to the village of Brisco. Turn left onto Brisco Road and reset your trip odometer. Drive down the hill and cross the railway tracks at 0.5 km. Turn right immediately after crossing the tracks. Cross the wetlands by a series of bridges. At 3.5 km keep right, staying on Brisco Road.

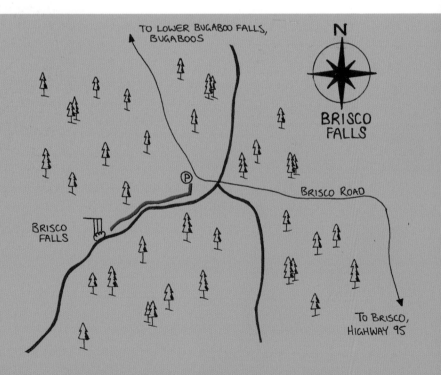

At 4.9 km cross a bridge (signed Klikwallie Bridge). Immediately after the bridge a road branches to the left. Park at either a widening at the junction or just past the intersection, on the right-hand side.

Hiking directions

From the intersection, pick up a boot-beaten trail leading into the trees near the creek. Use handmade wooden platforms to bypass a large rock outcropping. The falls will be visible from here. You can reach the base of the falls by skirting the creek on the right (slippery), by crossing on logs (also slippery) or simply wading through the water (probably slippery). All three options may be difficult during run-off or other periods of high stream flow. The falls can be visited from late April to late October but are best viewed from July to September once the water levels have dropped.

25. Bugaboo Falls (Lower)

LOCATION: Brisco
DRIVING DIFFICULTY: Moderate
HIKING DIFFICULTY: Easy
HIKING DISTANCE: 1.6 km
HIKING TIME: 30 min.

The glaciers of western Canada provide a steady supply of raw material which feeds these spectacular waterfalls. Follow Bugaboo Creek to its source and you'll find the Bugaboo Glacier tucked high amid the granite towers of Bugaboo Provincial Park. The result is a creek where runoff never really ends and water pumps ferociously late into the summer months.

Driving directions

From Radium, drive north on Highway 95 for about 20 minutes to the village of Brisco. Turn left onto Brisco Road and reset your trip odometer. Drive down the hill and over the railway tracks at 0.5 km. Turn right immediately after the tracks, and then cross the wetlands by a series of bridges. At 3.5 km keep right, staying on Brisco Road. At 8.4 km turn right onto Westside Road (signed). At 11.5 km there is a signed trailhead for Lower Bugaboo Falls Recreation Trail with a small parking area on the left.

Hiking directions

From the signed trailhead, follow a well-used and well-maintained trail on a treed plateau high above Bugaboo Creek. After about 20 minutes (1.3 km), the main trail forks down to the left (flagged), while another trail continues on to the edge of the canyon. The left fork is recommended for easier travel and will take you to a lookout near the top of the falls.

The right fork leads to the canyon edge, then drops down near the creek before regaining elevation steeply and reconnecting with the main trail. From the overlook at the top of the falls, you can backtrack along the edge of the canyon a short distance for a much better vista of a very impressive falls. Best viewed during runoff or periods of high stream flow, when the falls will be deafening. They can be accessed from April to late October, depending on snowfall.

N

LOWER
BUGABOO
FALLS

BUGABOO CREEK

WESTSIDE ROAD

P

TO BRISCO,
HIGHWAY 95

26. Bugaboo Falls

LOCATION: Brisco
DRIVING DIFFICULTY: Moderate
HIKING DIFFICULTY: Easy
HIKING DISTANCE: 100 m
HIKING TIME: about 78 seconds

This is one of the few trips in this book where the waterfall is not (or should not be) your final destination. Have a snack, use the loo, check out the falls and then set your sights on one of the many stunning routes that lie just ahead. Between the hike to the Bugaboos and Kain Basin, Cobalt Lake, Rocky Point Ridge, Silver Basin and Bugaboo Pass, there are enough quality trips to keep you busy for days.

Driving directions

Drive north of Radium on Highway 95 to the town of Brisco. Turn left onto Brisco Road and reset your trip odometer. Stay right at 3.5 km. Turn left at 8.5 km onto Brisco West Forestry Service Road (signed for Bugaboo Park and CMH Bugaboos). Turn right at 11.0 km onto Bugaboo Forestry Service Road (signed). Stay right at 22.5 km (signed). Stay right again at 24.4 km. Stay left at 27.3 km. At 41.1 km there is a wide pullout on the left signed for Upper Bugaboo Falls Recreation Site.

Hiking directions

Park the car. Follow well-used trails down to the creek and the base of the waterfall.

TO HIGHWAY 95, BRISCO

BUGABOO CREEK FORESTRY SERVICE ROAD

BUGABOO CREEK

N

UPPER BUGABOO FALLS

TO THE BUGABOOS

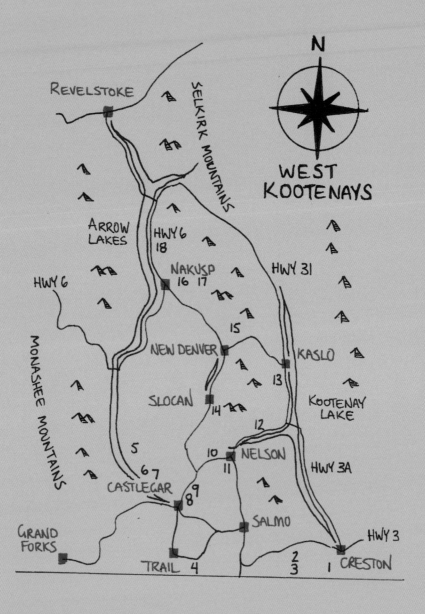

CHAPTER 2

West Kootenay

No matter where you go in the West Kootenay, you can expect to do it in relative solitude. Working your way deeper into BC's Southern Interior, you will find yourself farther from a major city, the hum of the Trans-Canada Highway and the masses of tourists. With that being said, the West Kootenay is increasingly becoming British Columbia's most poorly kept secret. This area is loaded with hidden gems of hikes, serene mountain lakes, hot springs and beautiful small towns.

The guidebook area covered is west of the Purcell Mountains, east of the Monashee Mountains, south of the Trans-Canada corridor and north of the United States border. The region is accessed by Highway 3 for travellers heading west from Cranbrook or east from the Okanagan. From the Trans-Canada, head south from Revelstoke on Highway 23 and cross Arrow Lake by way of the Shelter Bay ferry. A third, more remote option is east of Vernon via Highway 6 and the Needles Ferry.

Lakes are abundant in the West Kootenay, the by-product of hydroelectric damming on the Columbia and Kootenay river systems. Kootenay Lake, the Arrow Lakes and Slocan Lake offer many recreation opportunities for boating, fishing, camping and hiking. Although the town of Nelson is the major economic centre, with all the amenities of a big city, you will never be more than an hour from services as you navigate the long north to south valleys. Other service hubs include Creston, Trail, Castlegar, Nakusp and Kaslo.

When travelling around the region, it is important to plan ahead by checking ferry schedules in the summer and road conditions on the mountain passes in the winter. A missed ferry or a road closure for avalanche control can leave you idling for an hour or more.

1. Corn Creek Falls

LOCATION: Creston
DRIVING DIFFICULTY: Moderate
HIKING DIFFICULTY: Easy (see hiking directions)
HIKING DISTANCE: 400 m
HIKING TIME: 10 min.

The Creston valley is a small oasis in the Kootenays. While the rest of southeastern BC is still embraced in the cold throes of winter, Creston picks up an extra month of warm weather on either end of the colder season, allowing the snow to shed sooner and the valley's orchards to flourish. While driving through this town nestled between the Purcell and Selkirk mountains, it's only reasonable to expect that there are waterfalls to be had. Corn Creek Falls, although small, is a worthwhile outing and a beauty of a swimming hole in the summer months.

Driving directions

From the main intersection of Highways 3 and 3A in Creston, drive west on Highway 3 and cross the bridge over the wetlands. Turn left onto West Creston Road and reset your trip odometer. Turn right at 6.8 km and then a second immediate right onto Corn Creek Road. At 7.3 km stay right. Stay left at 8.5 km and then right at 8.9 km. The paved road ends at 9.7 km. At 11.3 km park in a wide, unsigned pullout on the right-hand side.

Hiking directions

From the parking area, pick up an unmarked trail into the trees on the right. The track descends gently at first and then steepens significantly, which can be slippery if wet or muddy. The route eventually nears the edge of a small canyon where the falls are obscured from sight below. If you backtrack slightly, you'll see a fixed rope leading down a short, steep gully to the creek at the base of the falls.

Note: I hesitate to recommend use of this rope, especially with small children. However, if you choose to subject your family to the final steps down to the creek, you'll be rewarded with a gorgeous, secluded swimming hole and a much better view of the small Corn Creek Falls.

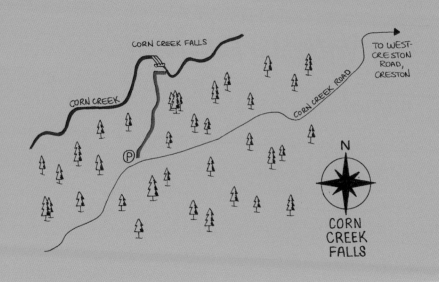

CORN CREEK FALLS

CORN CREEK

TO WEST-
CRESTON
ROAD,
CRESTON

CORN CREEK ROAD

N

CORN
CREEK
FALLS

More to explore

A more child-friendly option than the fixed rope to Corn Creek Falls is a stop at the Creston Valley Wildlife Management Area Interpretation Centre. Here you can take a canoe tour into the wetlands, walk the interpretive trails or grab your binoculars and try to identify the more than 300 species of birds that call the wetlands home.

2. North Star Falls (unofficial name)

LOCATION: Creston
DRIVING DIFFICULTY: Moderate
HIKING DIFFICULTY: Easy
HIKING DISTANCE: n/a
HIKING TIME: n/a

It's a small window to view North Star Falls, or whatever it's called, so get it while it's good. The road is not accessible until mid- to late May most years and the waterfall slows to a mere trickle later in the summer.

Driving directions

From the main intersection of Highways 3 and 3A in Creston, drive west on Highway 3 for 28 km. Turn left onto the Maryland Forest Service Road and reset your trip odometer. At 1.7 km stay right. At 2.6 km stay right, signed for Boundary Lake (brown pole). Stay left at 8.0 km. At 12.6 km stop. Look up and left! The falls are visible through the trees. The gravel road is unmaintained but generally in pretty good shape.

Hiking directions

There is no hiking to be had here, but this hidden cascade is a worthwhile stop on your way to Priest Falls or Boundary Lake. Best viewed earlier in the season or after a rainfall when more water is running.

More to explore

As a family, we have found that geo-caching is a great way to get the kids active in the outdoors and, more importantly, keep their interest level high. We have located geo-caches near many of the waterfalls in this book. The simplest way to describe geo-caching is to liken it to miniature treasure hunts, a useful description for convincing children of its merit. The downloadable smartphone application contains thousands of hidden caches all over the world. Some are simply

TO HIGHWAY 3, CRESTON

MARYLAND FORESTRY SERVICE ROAD

N

NORTH STAR FALLS

℗

TO PRIEST FALLS, BOUNDARY LAKE

tiny logbooks cleverly hidden from sight while others are larger canisters containing small items to swap. They are generally hidden using a natural feature, some disguised very well and others... a little too well!

3. Priest Falls

LOCATION: Creston
DRIVING DIFFICULTY: Moderate (see driving directions)
HIKING DIFFICULTY: Easy
HIKING DISTANCE: 1.8 km
HIKING TIME: 30 min.

Priest Falls is a hidden treasure in the Kootenay Pass area. Just north of the US border, before the Upper Priest River crosses the line, is a picturesque cascade tucked away in a maze of forestry roads and ATV trails. Combined with a trip to Boundary Lake, this is a great way to spend a day or even a weekend in the secluded corner of southeastern BC.

Driving directions

From the main intersection of Highways 3 and 3A in Creston, drive west on Highway 3 for 28 km. Turn left onto the Maryland Forest Service Road and reset your trip odometer. At 1.7 km stay right. At 2.6 km stay right at a recreation site sign for Boundary Lake (brown pole). Stay left at 8.0 km. At 13.4 stay left, again marked for Boundary Lake. At 16.3 km there is an unmarked intersection with an ATV trail and a wide area to park.

Note: with a high-clearance vehicle, you can drive 1.5 km down the ATV trail to a four-way junction. The road is rough, with pools of water, ruts and downed trees. Refer to the map for parking areas.

Hiking directions

From the original intersection with the ATV trail, hike along a rough and muddy ATV road for 1.5 km. At a four-way intersection take a left onto an even rougher ATV trail. Cross pools of water and deep ruts for 250 m to a small clearing in the trees and a viewpoint looking down on Priest Falls. A steep, slippery, boot-beaten trail descends to the base of the waterfall; take extra caution if choosing to travel below the viewpoint.

More to explore

There is a beautiful BC Recreation Site at Boundary Lake, just past the first parking area for Priest Falls. There are eleven campsites at this remote lake, making it a popular destination for paddling and ATVing in the summer months.

4. Beaver Falls

LOCATION: Fruitvale
DRIVING DIFFICULTY: Easy
HIKING DIFFICULTY: Easy
HIKING DISTANCE: 1.6 km
HIKING TIME: 30 min.

Without a formal trail, Beaver Falls is one of the lesser-known waterfalls in the area despite the Fruitvale "suburb" being named for the landmark.

Driving directions

From Fruitvale, drive west on Highway 3B to Bluebird Road. Pass the first couple of houses on the right-hand side and pull into a dirt parking area on the right, just before the train tracks.

doellphoto.com

Hiking directions

From the parking area, walk alongside the railway tracks for 1.6 km to the trestle over Beaver Creek. From this point you can look down on the stream as it plummets over a cliff below. A view of the falls can be achieved by dropping into the trees near the trestle downstream of the falls on the right-hand side. Take care, as the lightly used trail above the falls is quite steep and can be very slippery.

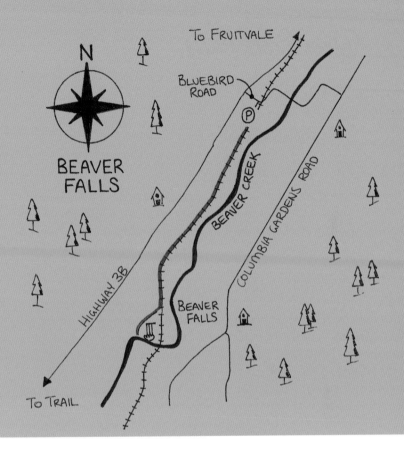

The Nelson & Fort Sheppard Railway

The tracks that you follow alongside of remain in use to this day. The route formerly extended all the way north to Nelson, but the section from Fruitvale to Nelson was decommissioned in the 1990s. The stretch of track that is currently in service runs between Atco Wood Products in Fruitvale to the US border. A couple of times per week, loaded railcars are moved south to forward products at the border.[4]

PHOTO: LARRY DOELL

5. Deer Creek Falls

LOCATION: Castlegar
DRIVING DIFFICULTY: Moderate
HIKING DIFFICULTY: Easy
HIKING DISTANCE: 1.0 km
HIKING TIME: 25 min.

This two-tiered waterfall is one of many along the north shore of Lower Arrow Lake. The lower of the two cascades is in plain sight and is worthwhile in itself, but with a little extra effort a look at the upper tier is a great reward.

Driving directions

From Castlegar, drive east on Highway 3A towards Nelson. Turn onto Robson Road shortly after crossing the Kootenay River and follow signs for Syringa Provincial Park. After 3.0 km turn right, onto Broadwater Road, and go 17.7 km to the Syringa Provincial Park campground. Near the campground entrance, stay right at the junction with the Deer Park Forest Service Road. Reset your trip odometer. At 13.4 km turn right, onto the Deer Creek Forest Service Road. At 16.9 km a brown recreation site pole on the left marks the parking area. Turn left and continue another 100 m to the signed trailhead and picnic area.

Hiking directions

From the trailhead, follow a well-used track through heavy forest. The route descends gently down towards the creek and follows along its right-hand side before coming to a picnic bench and a view of the lower falls. There are numerous downed logs in the vicinity of the base of the falls.

More to explore

Slightly hidden from sight is the upper tier of Deer Creek Falls. In the trees near the picnic bench there is a flagged and lightly boot-beaten trail which climbs up steeply to the right of the falls. The trails ends at a small lookout of the upper waterfall, or you can continue all the way to the creek above the waterfall. Take extra care if hiking past the main viewpoint at the picnic bench, though. A slip here could be costly, so this extension is not recommended with small children.

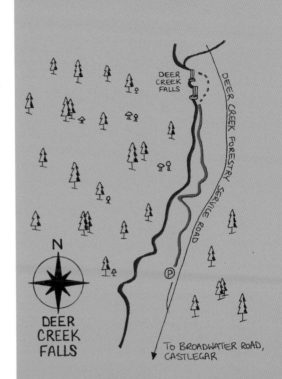

6. Cayuse Creek Waterslide

LOCATION: Syringa Provincial Park, Castlegar
DRIVING DIFFICULTY: Moderate
HIKING DIFFICULTY: Easy
HIKING DISTANCE: <100 m
HIKING TIME: <5 min.

Aptly named, the Cayuse Creek Waterslide is a popular swimming hole in the hot summer months. For those taking this ride, footwear is strongly recommended to access the top of the falls and then climb out afterwards. The rocks at the top and around the pool at the bottom are quite slippery. Sliding down the lower tier to the creek below is not recommended. Play safe!

Driving directions

From Castlegar, drive east on Highway 3A towards Nelson. Turn onto Robson Road shortly after crossing the Kootenay River and follow signs for Syringa Provincial Park. After 3.0 km, turn right, onto

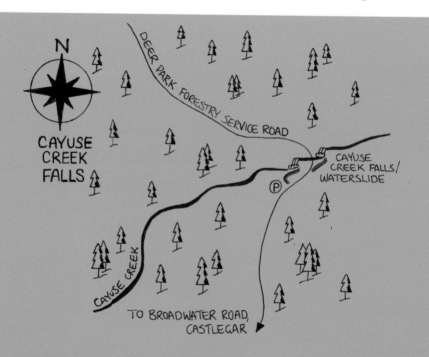

Broadwater Road, and go 17.7 km to the Syringa Provincial Park campground. Near the campground entrance, at a junction with the Deer Park Forest Service Road, stay right. Reset your trip odometer. At 10.9 km there is a pullout on the left, just before a bridge over Cayuse Creek. The bridge is directly over the upper tier of the falls.

Hiking directions

From the parking area there is a short, steep trail which takes you to the base of the upper tier of the falls. You can also cross the road to a steep trail which drops off behind the bridge. Use this to access the top of the waterslide.

7. Tulip Falls

LOCATION: Syringa Provincial Park, Castlegar
DRIVING DIFFICULTY: Moderate
HIKING DIFFICULTY: Easy
HIKING DISTANCE: 250 m
HIKING TIME: 5 min.

Tulip Falls is one of the most beautiful cascades in all of the West Kootenay, if not this entire guidebook. It is not a tall waterfall, nor does it have a large volume of water, yet the backdrop to Tulip Falls is truly striking. The approach enters a dark, narrow canyon where Tulip's delicate cascade is on display as it flows down moss-lined walls. Good luck capturing a bad photo of this one!

Driving directions

From Castlegar, drive east on Highway 3A towards Nelson. Turn onto Robson Road shortly after crossing the Kootenay River and follow signs for Syringa Provincial Park. After 3.0 km turn right, onto Broadwater Road, and go 17.7 km to the Syringa Provincial Park campground. Near the campground entrance, at a junction with the Deer Park Forest Service Road, stay right. Reset your trip odometer. At 3.9 km cross a bridge over Tulip Creek and park in an unsigned pullout on the right immediately after the bridge.

Hiking directions

From the parking area, follow a short, well-used trail on the left side of the creek to the base of the falls.

More to explore

Lower Arrow Lake and Syringa Provincial Park are popular summer destinations for recreation. There are numerous beaches, boat launches and marinas along Broadwater Road and into the park. While most people are content to soak in the sun on or near the lake, Tulip Falls offers a cool, shady retreat in the summer. The park is named for the syringa, also called "mock orange," which is a shrub native to the area.

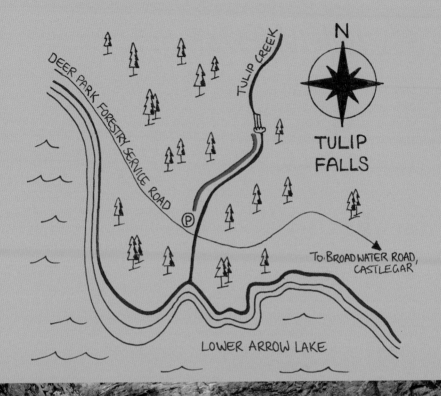

TULIP FALLS

DEER PARK FORESTRY SERVICE ROAD

TULIP CREEK

N

To BROADWATER ROAD, CASTLEGAR

LOWER ARROW LAKE

8. Little McPhee Falls

LOCATION: Castlegar
DRIVING DIFFICULTY: Moderate
HIKING DIFFICULTY: Easy
HIKING DISTANCE: 2.3 km
HIKING TIME: 45 min.

Little McPhee Falls is a small, beautiful waterfall tucked in a shady alcove fortified with mossy walls. If you've ever seen photos of people showering under a waterfall in the tropics and wished you could feel that exotic, this is a good place to make an attempt.

Driving directions

From Castlegar, drive east on Highway 3A towards Nelson. Turn right onto Ootischenia Road just north of the Castlegar airport. Reset your trip odometer. At 1.0 km turn left on Corrigan Road (signed for a golf course). At 1.3 km turn left onto Aaron Road. At 1.9 km turn right onto a gravel road (signed for McPhee Road). At 3.9 km stay left. At 5.6 km turn left down a dirt road (hiking/trailhead sign). Park at the signed trailhead at 5.9 km. There is a kiosk at the carpark with trail maps of the area. There is also an outhouse.

Hiking directions

From the trailhead, follow the signed Skattebo Reach Trail above the hydro station. At the first junction in the trail, trend right. The route travels on slopes high above the Kootenay River on a well-used and well-maintained trail. After about 1.5 km the trail begins to

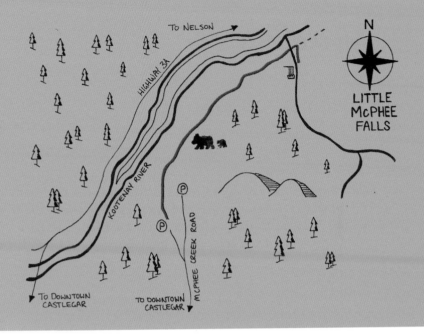

descend towards the river, gently at first and then more steeply before bottoming out at a bridge crossing Little McPhee Creek. Take a right immediately after the bridge (signed) and ascend briefly to the base of the falls.

This small, attractive waterfall cascades down a moss-covered wall. It is best to view it in spring and early summer before the streamflow becomes minimal later in the season.

Be bear aware

I had my closest run-in with a bear on this trail, and it serves as a strong reminder to not only know how to handle an encounter but also not to take your location for granted. You are in bear country in British Columbia whether you are two minutes from town or two days from the nearest road.

As I rounded an obstructed corner, I came across two bear cubs and ended up nearly directly between them and their mother. I had my bear spray in hand and instantly located the sow. I turned to face her, talking to her calmly but firmly. I raised my arms in the air, backed away slowly and waited until they moved on.

For more information on how to manage wildlife interactions, check out the introduction to this book and visit wildsafebc.com.

9. Glade Falls

LOCATION: Castlegar
DRIVING DIFFICULTY: Easy
HIKING DIFFICULTY: Easy
HIKING DISTANCE: 1.0 km
HIKING TIME: 20 min.

Glade Falls is a popular hideaway between Castlegar and Nelson. The fanfare is well deserved because the spot features easy access and a mellow stroll to a beautiful cascade, yet is just far enough off the beaten path to prevent it from becoming a total zoo.

Driving directions

From Castlegar, drive east on Highway 3A towards Nelson for about 10 minutes. Across from an Esso station, turn right, onto Glade Ferry Road. Follow this road down to the Kootenay River and take the three-minute ferry ride across. Once on the other side, take your first right, onto Glade Road, and follow it to the end of pavement. Park in a wide turnaround.

Hiking directions

This area is a mishmash of dirt roads, ATV trails and paths going off in every direction. The easiest route follows an ATV trail. From the parking area, walk up the dirt road and cross a bridge after about 200 m. Another 100 m farther, take the ATV trail to the left, which gently gains elevation as it trends away from the creek before heading back towards it. After about 15 minutes the ATV trail will bend hard to the right just as the waterfall can be heard. At this point, pick up a well-used footpath into the trees to the base of the falls.

Know before you go

The Glade Ferry across the Kootenay River is a cable vessel that runs on demand from 5:00 am to 2:20 am daily. A new ferry, *Glade II*, was put into service in January 2018 and can handle up to ten vehicles at a time. The free crossing takes about three minutes.

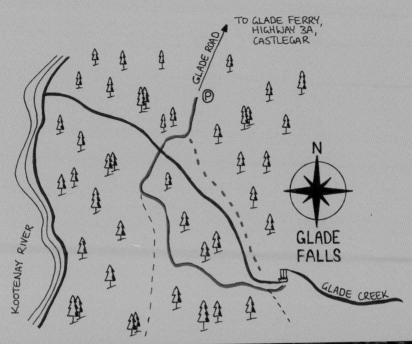

TO GLADE FERRY, HIGHWAY 3A, CASTLEGAR

GLADE ROAD

GLADE FALLS

GLADE CREEK

KOOTENAY RIVER

10. Sproule Creek Falls

LOCATION: Nelson
DRIVING DIFFICULTY: Easy
HIKING DIFFICULTY: Easy
HIKING DISTANCE: 400 m
HIKING TIME: 10 min.

It is always fun to highlight little hidden gems that even locals are sometimes unaware of. Sproule Creek Falls is a great example. While it is a small waterfall, the narrow gap in the cliffs it slips through makes it a worthwhile sight in a unique setting.

Driving directions

From Nelson, drive west on Highway 3A towards Castlegar. Reset your trip odometer at the intersection of Highways 6 and 3A. Cross a bridge over the Kootenay River. At 7.2 km turn right onto Reibin Road. Drive down the hill, dodging potholes and humps, and pull into an unmarked parking area on the left just before the bridge.

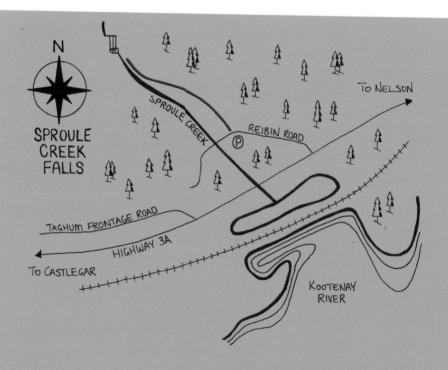

Hiking directions

From the parking area, cross the road and pick up a faint trail upstream of the bridge. The boot-beaten track travels up the right-hand side of the creek and passes briefly through a grassy clearing before entering the trees. A couple of delicate steps across the top of a boulder deliver you to a secluded little waterfall tucked into a narrow canyon lined with steep rock walls.

Note: This route runs adjacent to private land. Please stay on the established trail and respect the property of nearby landowners.

11. Cottonwood Falls

LOCATION: Nelson
DRIVING DIFFICULTY: Easy
HIKING DIFFICULTY: Easy
HIKING DISTANCE: 100 m
HIKING TIME: 2-ish min.

This is as simple as it gets, folks: a beautiful waterfall right in town with a walk that takes less time than ordering a double-double at a coffee shop drive-through. Cottonwood Park makes a great picnic area if you're spending the day in the Nelson area and is a quiet refuge away from the busy downtown streets.

Driving directions

Located in Cottonwood Park, the falls are a beautiful escape right in town. From downtown Nelson, take Baker Street west across Highway 3A. Turn left onto Railway Street just before the A&W. Take your

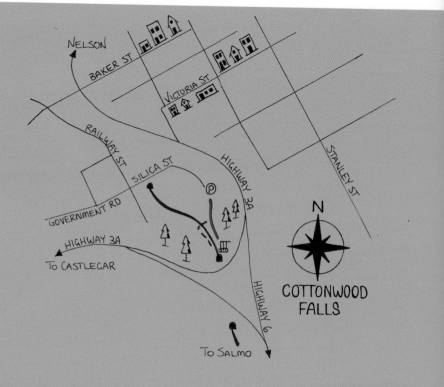

next left onto Silica Street behind the Ford dealership. Park in the gravel parking area at Cottonwood Park.

Hiking directions

A quick stroll into the park takes you to the base of Cottonwood Falls. You can also cross the bridge in the park and access the falls from the opposite side of the creek.

More to explore

No, not more trails! I'm talking about the food and restaurant scene in Nelson. This town has more fantastic places to eat per capita than anywhere in the Kootenays. I won't make any recommendations other than to try them all!

12. Canyon Falls

LOCATION: Kokanee Creek Provincial Park, Nelson
DRIVING DIFFICULTY: Easy
HIKING DIFFICULTY: Easy
HIKING DISTANCE: 1.0 km
HIKING TIME: 25 min.

Kokanee is the Sinixt word for the red fish that swim upstream to spawn, and in late August and September the spawning channels in Kokanee Creek Provincial Park are teeming with them. The park is popular with locals and tourists alike for its plentiful camping, beaches, boating, and hiking trails. One such hike is the Canyon Trail, which winds its way upstream of the lake through old-growth cedar and fir forests to a lookout high above Kokanee Creek as Canyon Falls spills through a narrow, rocky canyon.

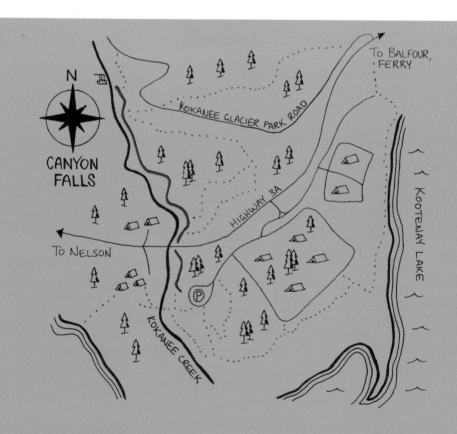

Driving directions

From downtown Nelson, drive east on Highway 3A towards the Balfour ferry terminal. Kokanee Creek Provincial Park is 21 km from town, a 20- to 25-minute drive along the winding road on the north shore of Kootenay Lake. Turn into the signed park entrance. Drive past the campground kiosk and turn right for the visitor centre, where parking is available.

Hiking directions

From the main parking area, pick up the trail leading upstream on the right-hand side of the creek, signed for Canyon Trail. Cross under the highway and follow the signs on the well-used trail. After 1 km (about 20 minutes) there is a sign for Canyon Lookout. The trail climbs briefly before descending a set of stairs to a platform overlooking Kokanee Creek as it drops multiple times before entering a narrow canyon.

Know before you go

Please check seasonal trail closures. Bears are known to frequent the park and the spawning channels in late summer and early autumn. Dogs are often prohibited during closures to help prevent wildlife encounters. Check trailhead signage and postings at the visitor centre before heading out on trails in the park.

13. Fletcher Falls

LOCATION: Kaslo
DRIVING DIFFICULTY: Easy
HIKING DIFFICULTY: Easy
HIKING DISTANCE: 300 m
HIKING TIME: 10 min.

Fletcher Falls is one of the most picturesque in the West Kootenays and its reputation is well deserved. The dark, mossy canyon is encircled with stately cedars, providing the backdrop to this beautiful waterfall. In the summer months, the parking area is often overflowing with visitors flocking to what has become a landmark along Kootenay Lake near Kaslo.

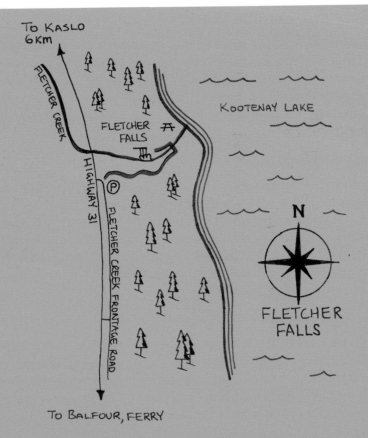

Driving directions

From Kaslo, drive 6 km south on Highway 31. Turn left onto Fletcher Creek Frontage Road, which can be accessed from two points off the highway. The trailhead is at the far north end of the road. Park on the shoulder, taking care not to block the driveways of the private residences. If travelling from Nelson or the Balfour ferry, drive 26 km north from the ferry terminal, on Highway 31.

Hiking directions

Pick up the signed trailhead for the Fletcher Falls Recreation Trail at the north end of Fletcher Creek Frontage Road. The trail is generally quite busy from spring through fall. It descends moderately to near the lakeshore before crossing a bridge and returning upstream to the base of the falls. Numerous steep shortcuts exist on the way down, providing nice views of the falls from above. Take care near the edge of the canyon, especially after a good rain. There are picnic benches and lake access at the bottom of the trail.

14. Springer Creek Falls

LOCATION: Slocan
DRIVING DIFFICULTY: Easy
HIKING DIFFICULTY: Easy
HIKING DISTANCE: 200 m
HIKING TIME: 5 min.

Slocan boasts a gem of a campground just on the outskirts of the small town. If two-ply toilet paper in the outhouses isn't incentive enough, there is also one of the Kootenays' most attractive waterfalls tucked away in the heart of the campground!

Driving directions

The Springer Creek Campground is located in the village of Slocan just off Highway 6. At the campground entrance there is a picnic and parking area near the office and visitor information centre.

Hiking directions

From the picnic/parking area, numerous trails wind through the campground, but the easiest way is to stay left on the road that descends to the lower loop of the campground. The waterfall will just be visible on the right through the trees. The base of it is easily accessed via a boot-beaten trail on the right-hand side of the creek. Additional trails throughout the campground lead to a footbridge which looks down over Springer Creek from above the falls.

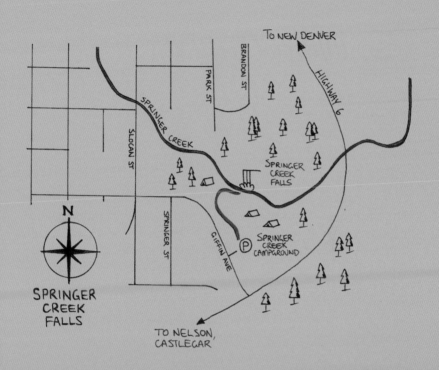

SPRINGER
CREEK
FALLS

To New Denver

Highway 6

Park St

Brandon St

Springer Creek

Sloan St

Springer Creek Falls

Springer St

Giffin Ave

Springer Creek Campground

To Nelson, Castlegar

N

15. Wilson Creek Falls

LOCATION: New Denver
DRIVING DIFFICULTY: Moderate
HIKING DIFFICULTY: Easy
HIKING DISTANCE: 1.2 km
HIKING TIME: 25 min.

When picturing waterfalls in the Kootenays, something resembling the behemoth on Wilson Creek usually comes to mind. Fuelled by glaciers high above in Goat Range Provincial Park, this cascade surges with an obscene amount of force long after the spring run-off has ended. Expect to get your clothes, your camera gear and your kids wet as you approach it at the end of the trail. Wilson Creek is a beast of a waterfall and impressive at any time of year. The roar of it is thunderous and can be heard long before the cataract itself becomes visible.

Driving directions

From the intersection of Highways 6 and 31A in New Denver, drive north on Highway 6 for 5.4 km. Turn right onto Wilson Creek Road East. Reset your trip odometer. At 1 km, cross the bridge where the pavement ends. Ignore all driveways, branches and spur roads on your right. Follow a good gravel road for 11.5 km and turn right (signed for Wilson Creek Falls). The next 700 m to the trailhead are a little rougher but manageable in a car. Park at the signed trailhead.

Hiking directions

From the trailhead, a well-used route travels through the trees and gains elevation slightly before descending moderately to the base of the falls. Before the trail starts descending, another trail branches off to the right (orange markers in trees and log across trail), which can be ignored. Descend via the main trail to the left. The spray from the falls carries a long way and can make the lower trail slippery at any time of year.

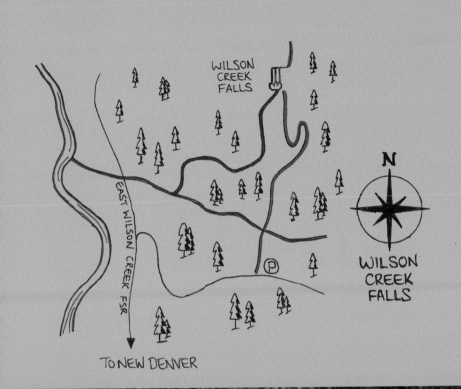

WILSON CREEK FALLS

N

WILSON CREEK FALLS

EAST WILSON CREEK FSR

TO NEW DENVER

16. Gardner Creek Falls

LOCATION: Nakusp
DRIVING DIFFICULTY: Easy
HIKING DIFFICULTY: Easy
HIKING DISTANCE: n/a
HIKING TIME: n/a

In case you need a second reason to drive up the road to Nakusp Hot Springs, this gorgeous roadside waterfall is it. Or, in case you need a second reason to drive up the road to Gardner Creek Falls, Nakusp Hot Springs is it. Either way, you won't be disappointed.

Driving directions

From the junction of Highways 23 and 6 in Nakusp, drive north on Highway 23 for 1.0 km and turn right onto Hot Springs Road. Reset your trip odometer. Drive towards Nakusp Hot Springs for 8.3 km

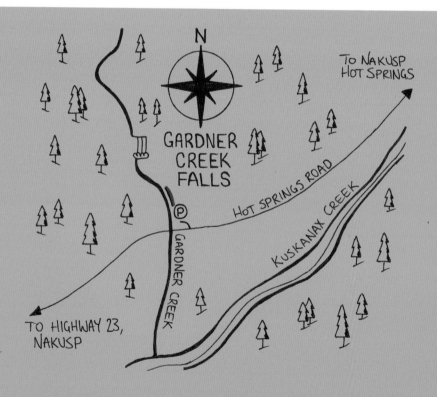

to a bridge over Gardner Creek. There are pullouts on the left before and after the bridge. The best view of the falls is from the pullout after crossing the bridge.

Hiking directions

Gardner Creek Falls is a beauty, and although it is tough to get closer to it than the creek's bank near the parking area, it is equally tough to improve on the view from that point. The road is maintained year-round, allowing visitors to take in the falls and soak in the hot springs just up the road.

17. Kuskanax Falls

LOCATION: Nakusp
DRIVING DIFFICULTY: Easy
HIKING DIFFICULTY: Easy
HIKING DISTANCE: 450 m
HIKING TIME: 10 min.

The waterfall on Kuskanax Creek will almost certainly be overshadowed by the many other highlights on the road from Nakusp, including Gardner Creek Falls, the Hot Springs and the impressive covered timber-frame bridge over the creek. The waterfall is not large, and even during periods of high stream flow it would be difficult to describe it as a waterfall. But if you are looking for a secluded short hike off the beaten path and away from the crowds, this is the place to do it.

Driving directions

From the junction of Highways 23 and 6 in Nakusp, drive north on Highway 23 for 1 km and turn right onto Hot Springs Road. Drive to Nakusp Hot Springs. At the end of the road (12 km) is the main parking area and a signed trailhead for Hot Springs Trail. Park here.

Hiking directions

From the signed trailhead, follow a large, well-used trail for 300 m to an ornate covered wooden bridge. Immediately after crossing the bridge, take the lesser used left fork and follow it for another 150 m to a rocky overlook above Kuskanax Creek and a small but powerful waterfall. The spray during runoff or after a good rain makes it tricky to stay dry while taking a photo.

Nakusp Hot Springs

Nakusp Hot Springs is one of the lesser known in southeastern BC compared to some of the others in the region such as Halcyon (just up the highway), Canyon Hot Springs near Revelstoke, or Radium and Fairmont in the East Kootenays. Being a little farther removed from a major highway, Nakusp is a much more relaxing hot spring experience.

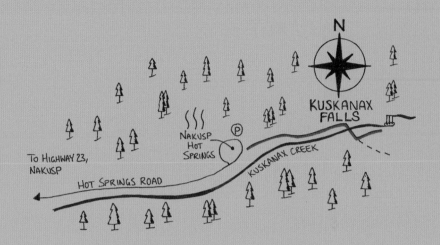

N

KUSKANAX
FALLS

To Highway 23,
NAKUSP

Nakusp
Hot
Springs

P

HOT SPRINGS ROAD

KUSKANAX CREEK

18. Ione Falls

LOCATION: Nakusp
DRIVING DIFFICULTY: Easy
HIKING DIFFICULTY: Easy
HIKING DISTANCE: n/a
HIKING TIME: n/a

A jaw-dropping waterfall so easy to access even your chihuahua can get out of the car to steal a view of this beautiful cascade.

Driving directions

From the intersection of Highways 23 and 6 in Nakusp, drive north on Highway 23 along Upper Arrow Lake for 19.5 km to a signed rest area. Pull over into a parking lot on the right. The falls are around the corner, just out of sight and only briefly visible from the highway.

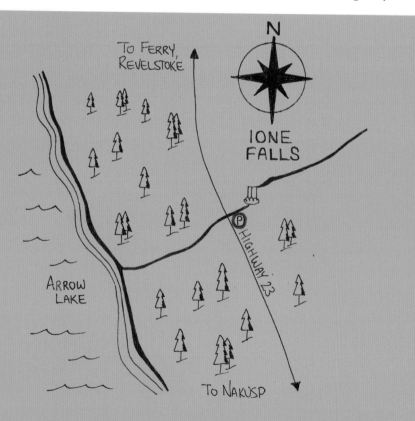

Hiking directions

Step out of your car and take 50 paces to the base of one of the most picturesque waterfalls in the province. That is all.

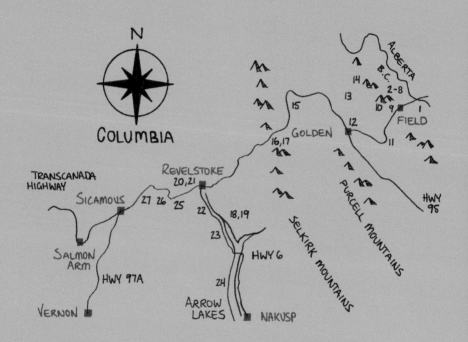

CHAPTER 3

Trans-Canada Corridor / Columbia

Amid the chaos of the Formula One racetrack the Trans-Canada Highway has become, there are many hidden escapes tucked just out of sight from the snaking motorway. Waterfalls are plentiful along the country's busiest highway as it winds through the Rocky Mountains and then westward through the Purcell, Selkirk and Monashee ranges. The high glaciers that cling to these landmarks fuel the creeks, rivers and waterfalls year-round. While many become inaccessible during the winter months, numerous falls around Revelstoke are sufficiently close to the highway and at low enough elevations that they can be reached even when the snow flies.

The region detailed in this section extends from the BC/Alberta boundary in Yoho National Park down to Golden, through Glacier National Park and west through Revelstoke to Sicamous. Services and accommodation are available in towns along the Trans-Canada, including Field, Golden, Revelstoke and Sicamous. The drive is highlighted by the spectacular, world-renowned scenery throughout Yoho and Glacier national parks as well as numerous provincial parks and recreation sites. It is easy to see why people from around the world flock to this region!

1. Seven Veils Falls

LOCATION: Yoho National Park
DRIVING DIFFICULTY: Easy
HIKING DIFFICULTY: Easy
HIKING DISTANCE: 1.5 km (to falls via Lake O'Hara Shoreline Trail)
HIKING TIME: 30 min.

Seven Veils Falls is a gorgeous waterfall but will undoubtedly be overshadowed by the many iconic vistas in the Lake O'Hara region of Yoho National Park. While it would be easy to overlook these cascades as you explore the area, a stop along the Lake O'Hara shoreline to admire this waterfall is a must!

Driving directions

From Field, drive east on the Trans-Canada Highway towards the BC/Alberta boundary. Turn right, into the parking area signed for Lake O'Hara. If you are one of the lucky few to secure a seat on the bus, a campsite at the lake or a spot in the Alpine Club of Canada's Elizabeth Parker Hut, you'd best be counting your blessings. Lake O'Hara has become one of the most sought-after outdoor playgrounds in Canada, much to the dismay of local backcountry enthusiasts.

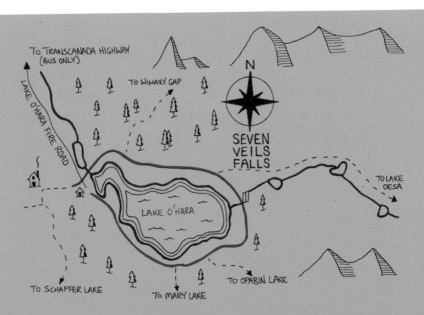

Hiking directions

If you aren't so fortunate as to get a spot on the bus, don't worry! You can still hike the 11 km road in. Once you reach the lake, whether on foot or by way of Parks's luxurious chauffeur service, locate the trailhead kiosk near the bus stop. Cross Cataract Brook and wind around the lake in a clockwise direction, following signs for Lake Oesa. At a junction at the far end of the lake, stay low and right; Seven Veils Falls is a short distance beyond. The Lake O'Hara shoreline trail is a 2.8 km circuit from the trailhead where the bus stops. Seven Veils Falls is roughly at the halfway point.

More to explore

Let's face it, you didn't come here for a waterfall. You came to Lake O'Hara to experience one of the natural wonders of this country. The trail network around Lake O'Hara can take you high into the alpine where deep blue lakes sit peacefully at the base of some of the tallest and most majestic mountains in the Rockies. Expertly crafted pathways meander around alpine tarns and meadows. Climb stone staircases and cling to butt-puckering ledges as you tour the alpine high above the bustling base camp near the lakeshore. This may be the closest thing to heaven an earthbound person could envision.

PHOTO: DONYANE DOMAM, DREAMSTIME.COM

2. Whiskey Jack Falls

LOCATION: Yoho National Park
DRIVING DIFFICULTY: Easy
HIKING DIFFICULTY: Easy
HIKING DISTANCE: n/a
HIKING TIME: n/a

Whiskey Jack Falls is only a sample of what is to come when exploring the Yoho Valley. You will be surrounded by some of the classic Canadian Rockies hikes, including the famed Iceline Trail and the historic Yoho Valley Trail to Twin Falls. Don't plan to spend much time ogling this waterfall, as greater sights are only a short distance beyond.

Driving directions

From Field, drive east on the Trans-Canada Highway for 3.5 km and turn onto the signed Yoho Valley Road. Follow for 13.0 km to just before the Takakkaw Falls parking area. Note that the parking on the left is only for people staying at the Whiskey Jack Hostel. The falls are visible from the roadway.

Hiking directions

You don't have to get out of your car to see Whiskey Jack Falls unless human congestion requires you to park on the road at this point. Snap a photo from here and keep going to the main parking area. You won't be able to get too much closer to the falls anyway, even if starting one of the many day hikes in the area at this trailhead.

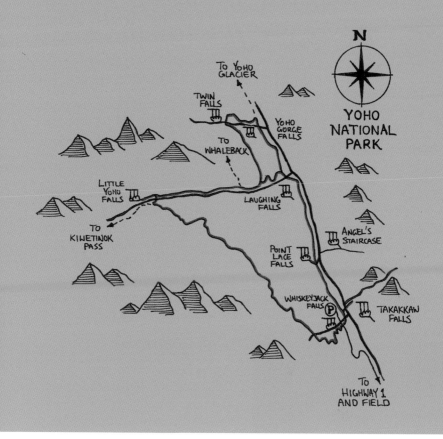

Know before you go

A park pass is required to stop on the Yoho Valley Road. Passes can be purchased at the visitor centres in Field, Radium, Lake Louise or Banff and at the highway kiosks for Kootenay and Banff national parks. If coming up to the Takakkaw Falls / Yoho Valley area, be sure to arrive early to get parking. This is one of the most popular day use and backpacking areas in the Rockies once the Yoho Valley Road opens in late June.

3. Takakkaw Falls

LOCATION: Yoho National Park
DRIVING DIFFICULTY: Easy
HIKING DIFFICULTY: Easy
HIKING DISTANCE: 600 m
HIKING TIME: 10 min.

As you round the final curves of the Yoho Valley Road your gaze is likely to shift up and right. Your eyes will go wide and your jaw will slowly assume the "dropped" position. That, my friends, is Takakkaw Falls, one of the most impressive cascades in this country, if not in all of North America. The iconic rooster tail of the upper portion launches glacial meltwater nearly 400 vertical metres to the valley floor below. This is one of the truly spectacular scenes you will experience in your lifetime and one that you will not soon forget!

Driving directions

From Field, drive east on the Trans-Canada Highway for 3.5 km and turn onto the signed Yoho Valley Road. Continue for 13.5 km to the Takakkaw Falls parking area. Signed trailhead kiosks mark the Takakkaw Falls hike as well as the Yoho Valley trails. There are washroom facilities and picnic areas around the parking lot.

Hiking directions

From the signed trailhead, follow the large gravel pathway along the Yoho River with the falls towering above you. After about 200 m take the bridge across the river and follow the trail towards the base of the one of the most awe-inspiring waterfalls in the country.

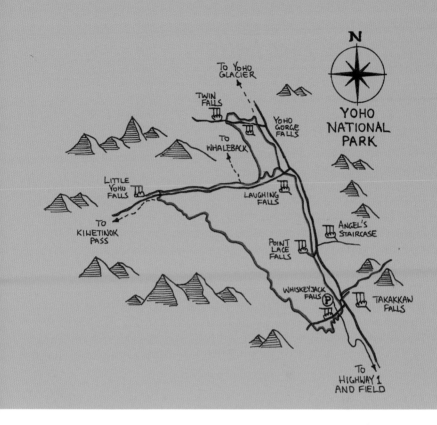

Another viewing option is to hike the steep trail to the Yoho Iceline. The trailhead for this is near the Whiskey Jack Hostel and the route is unrelenting before breaking treeline at a rocky alpine area. This option would be considered difficult due to the elevation gain, but the views across the valley to Takakkaw Falls are breathtaking.

Know before you go

According to Parks Canada, Takakkaw Falls drops a total of 384 m, making it the second tallest waterfall in the country after Della Falls on Vancouver Island. Takakkaw is a Cree word that expresses awe and wonder.

4. Point Lace Falls

LOCATION: Yoho National Park
DRIVING DIFFICULTY: Easy
HIKING DIFFICULTY: Easy
HIKING DISTANCE: 2.7 km
HIKING TIME: 45 min.

Point Lace Falls is often overlooked by hikers hell-bent on reaching Twin Falls or the Little Yoho Valley. Oh well, their loss. This is an elegant cascade tucked just out of sight from the Yoho Valley "super highway," and chances are you will enjoy it in solitude.

Driving directions

From Field, drive east on the Trans-Canada Highway for 3.5 km and turn onto the signed Yoho Valley Road. Continue for 13.5 km to the Takakkaw Falls parking area. Signed trailhead kiosks mark the Takakkaw Falls hike as well as the Yoho Valley trails. There are washroom facilities and picnic areas around the parking lot.

Hiking directions

Point Lace Falls is a beautiful cascade situated along the Yoho Valley trail and is often overlooked in favour of the more recognizable waterfalls. From the signed trailhead, follow directions for Laughing Falls. You will hike through the walk-in campground along a large gravel trail. At 2.5 km there is a signed junction for Point Lace Falls to your left, Laughing Falls further ahead and Angel's Staircase to the right. Leave the main trail and follow a short spur for 200 m to the base of the falls.

More to explore

Near the junction of the main Yoho Valley trail and Point Lace Falls is a second short detour to a viewpoint of the Angel's Staircase. From a distance, this stream can be seen cartwheeling down the entire mountainside in a series of steps before its eventual confluence with the Yoho River. The Staircase is best viewed with binoculars or with a telephoto lens on your camera.

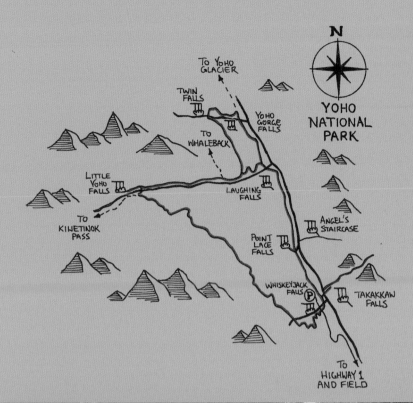

N

YOHO
NATIONAL
PARK

TO YOHO
GLACIER

TWIN
FALLS

YOHO GORGE
FALLS

TO
WHALEBACK

LITTLE
YOHO FALLS

LAUGHING
FALLS

TO
KIWETINOK
PASS

ANGEL'S
STAIRCASE

POINT
LACE
FALLS

WHISKEYJACK
FALLS

TAKAKKAW
FALLS

TO
HIGHWAY 1
AND FIELD

5. Laughing Falls

LOCATION: Yoho National Park
DRIVING DIFFICULTY: Easy
HIKING DIFFICULTY: Easy
HIKING DISTANCE: 4.6 km
HIKING TIME: 1.5 hrs.

Laughing Falls is occasionally overshadowed by other attractions in the Yoho Valley, including Takakkaw Falls, Twin Falls and the Iceline Trail. Yet, if this waterfall were anywhere else, it would have massive appeal all on its own with its easy access and a backcountry campground within a stone's throw. The cascade stands more than 30 m tall and relentlessly propels the waters of Little Yoho Creek year-round. It is visible from the main Yoho Valley trail, making it a great lunch spot for backpackers heading to the Twin Falls or Little Yoho campgrounds. It can be a great objective in itself or simply a spot to lay over.

Driving directions

From Field, drive east on the Trans-Canada Highway for 3.5 km and turn onto the signed Yoho Valley Road. Continue for 13.5 km to the Takakkaw Falls parking area. Signed trailhead kiosks mark the Takakkaw Falls hike as well as the Yoho Valley trails. There are washroom facilities and picnic areas around the parking lot.

Hiking directions

From the Takakkaw Falls parking area, follow the well-used and well-marked trail to Laughing Falls. The route gains very little elevation over the first 2.5 km to the junction of Angel's Staircase and Point Lace Falls. After the junction the trail narrows slightly and gains modest elevation for the next 2 km before crossing a bridge over the Little Yoho River. The impressive falls are visible on your left; the Laughing Falls campground is on the right.

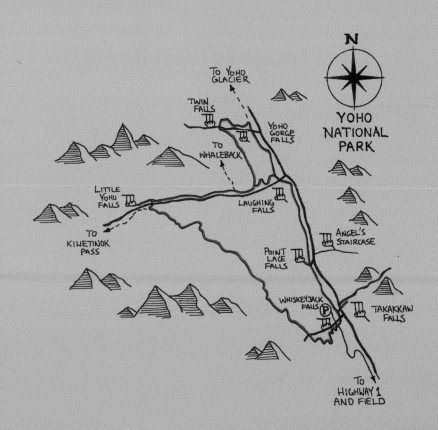

N

YOHO
NATIONAL
PARK

TO YOHO
GLACIER

TWIN
FALLS

YOHO
GORGE
FALLS

TO
WHALEBACK

LITTLE
YOHO
FALLS

LAUGHING
FALLS

TO
KIWETINOK
PASS

ANGEL'S
STAIRCASE

POINT
LACE
FALLS

WHISKEYJACK
FALLS

TAKAKKAW
FALLS

TO
HIGHWAY 1
AND FIELD

6. Yoho Gorge / Marpole Falls (unofficial name)

LOCATION: Yoho National Park
DRIVING DIFFICULTY: Easy
HIKING DIFFICULTY: Moderate
HIKING DISTANCE: 7.3 km
HIKING TIME: 2.5–3 hr.

It seems Twin Falls has effectively stolen the show from this little-known feature along the Yoho Valley trail. Available resources have referenced this narrow gorge as both Yoho Gorge Falls and Marpole Falls, but it is not shown in any Parks Canada mapping or trail descriptions. But don't let that stop you from dropping your pack and pulling out the camera once you arrive.

Driving directions

From Field, drive east on the Trans-Canada Highway for 3.5 km and turn onto the signed Yoho Valley Road. Continue for 13.5 km to the Takakkaw Falls parking area. Signed trailhead kiosks mark the Takakkaw Falls hike as well as the Yoho Valley trails. There are washroom facilities and picnic areas around the parking lot.

Hiking directions

Hike the well-maintained and signed Yoho Valley Trail for 7 km to the Twin Falls campground. Along the way you will pass the Angel's Staircase viewpoint, Point Lace Falls, Laughing Falls and the junction for the Little Yoho Valley. Once through the Twin Falls campground, the trail starts to gain elevation moderately to Twin Falls and the site of the historic Twin Falls Chalet. Along the trail on the left, the mouth of the gorge is just visible near a picnic bench. You can wiggle through the trees for a better look of the creek as it slips down and out of the narrow canyon.

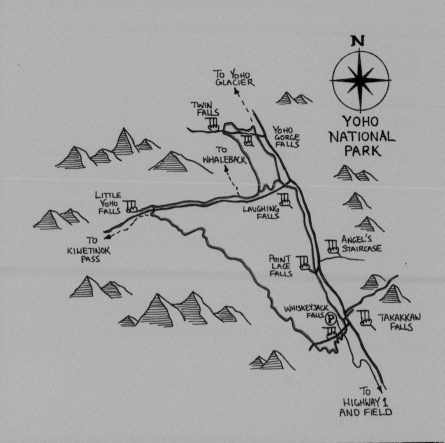

N

YOHO NATIONAL PARK

TO YOHO GLACIER

TWIN FALLS

YOHO GORGE FALLS

TO WHALEBACK

LITTLE YOHO FALLS

LAUGHING FALLS

TO KIWETINOK PASS

ANGEL'S STAIRCASE

POINT LACE FALLS

WHISKEYJACK FALLS

TAKAKKAW FALLS

TO HIGHWAY 1 AND FIELD

7. Twin Falls

LOCATION: Yoho National Park, BC
DRIVING DIFFICULTY: Easy
HIKING DIFFICULTY: Moderate
HIKING DISTANCE: 8.4 km
HIKING TIME: 3 hr.

Decision time: what do you explore first? The site of the historic Twin Falls Chalet? Or the trails around this postcard-worthy waterfall? If that decision is the hardest thing you have to do upon reaching the falls, you're probably having a fantastic day.

Driving directions

From Field, drive east on the Trans-Canada Highway for 3.5 km and turn onto the signed Yoho Valley Road. Continue for 13.5 km to the Takakkaw Falls parking area. Signed trailhead kiosks mark the Takakkaw Falls hike as well as the Yoho Valley Trails. There are washroom facilities and picnic areas around the parking lot.

Hiking directions

A well-used and well-marked trail for Twin Falls follows alongside the Yoho River and initially gains minimal elevation. After passing through the Laughing Falls campsite at 4.6 km, cross the Yoho River and continue to the Twin Falls campsite at 7.0 km. The trail then gains moderate elevation to the site of the Twin Falls Chalet. A small loop from the building takes you to a series of viewpoints of the iconic Twin Falls. Another trail gains elevation steeply to the top of the waterfall.

It does make for a long day hike, especially with the addition of travel to and from the trailhead. However, with multiple campgrounds in the valley, the Alpine Club of Canada's Stanley Mitchell Hut and the Chalet itself, there are many ways to slow the pace and extend the trip over several days.

The Twin Falls Chalet

Construction of the iconic structure by the Canadian Pacific Railway began in 1908. The main lodge was completed in 1923 and opened

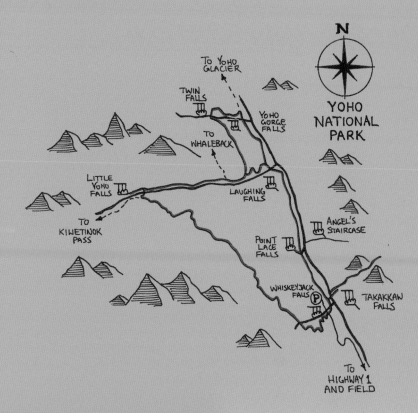

the following year. It was operated as a tea house by CP Rail through the 1950s until rail-based tourism dropped off. It reopened in 1959 for backcountry accommodation and operated from 1962 to 2019 under the watchful eye of Fran Drummond.[5]

8. Little Yoho Falls (unofficial name)

LOCATION: Yoho National Park
DRIVING DIFFICULTY: Easy
HIKING DIFFICULTY: Moderate
HIKING DISTANCE: 10.2 km
HIKING TIME: 3.5–4.5 hr.

It shouldn't be a shock to find out there is yet another waterfall to explore in the Yoho Valley. What might be a surprise is that it's tucked away just out the back door of the Little Yoho campground. How many people have enjoyed this campsite – cooking meals, filtering water from the creek or just good old-fashioned freezing in their sleeping bags – and all the while a pretty little waterfall was right around the corner?

Driving directions

From Field, drive east on the Trans-Canada Highway for 3.5 km and turn onto the signed Yoho Valley Road. Continue for 13.5 km to the Takakkaw Falls parking area. Signed trailhead kiosks mark the Takakkaw Falls hike as well as the Yoho Valley trails. There are washrooms and picnic areas around the parking lot.

Hiking directions

From the signed trailhead, follow the Yoho Valley Trail to Laughing Falls at 4.6 km. Cross the bridge over the Little Yoho River, pass the Laughing Falls campground and take a left at the junction signed for Little Yoho and Stanley Mitchell Hut. The trail gains moderate elevation over the next 5.0 km to Mitchell Hut. Follow the trail for an additional 200 m to the Little Yoho Campground. Walk through the campground past the food poles and pick up a boot-beaten trail down to the river. A small waterfall is tucked away just out of sight past the far end of the campground.

A second fall is another 200 m beyond this point. Follow the faint trail up and past the lower falls. Step with care, as the trail briefly sideslopes across a steep, loose roll before delivering you to a larger upper cascade. The waterfall is not noted on any Parks Canada maps or resources, making it a beautiful and quiet spot to hide out. Take the extra five minutes and go explore!

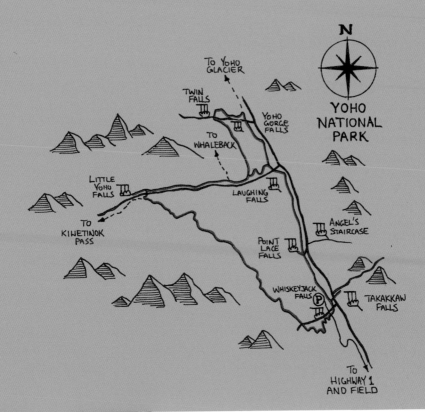

More to explore

The Little Yoho campground and Stanley Mitchell Hut make great base camps to explore the world famous Iceline Trail as well as side trips to Kiwetinok Pass, Kiwetinok Lake and the Whaleback. For the more adventurous there are numerous scrambling and mountaineering opportunities afoot.

Reservations for the Little Yoho campground can be made through Parks Canada, while a spot in the Stanley Mitchell Hut can be booked through the Alpine Club of Canada. If you are fortunate enough to secure a reservation, you will be well rewarded with the chance to enjoy one of the most stunning areas in the Canadian Rockies.

129

9. Natural Bridge

LOCATION: Yoho National Park
DRIVING DIFFICULTY: Easy
HIKING DIFFICULTY: Easy
HIKING DISTANCE: <100 m
HIKING TIME: <5min

One of the most recognizable photos from the Canadian national parks is the raging Kickinghorse River being squeezed through the eye of a needle under the Natural Bridge. Its close proximity to the Trans-Canada Highway, accessible pathways and unique setting make it one of the busiest pit stops in all of western Canada. This landmark is spectacular during any season!

Driving directions

From Field, drive west on the Trans-Canada Highway for 1.5 km and turn right onto the signed Emerald Lake Road. Follow Emerald Lake Road for 2.5 km to a busy parking area on the left signed for the Natural Bridge.

Hiking directions

Walk to a lookout atop a small chasm where you can view the Kickinghorse River just before it is forced through a narrow slot in the rocks. Alternatively, you can take the bridge across the river for a view of the water leaving the narrow opening. The Natural Bridge is a very unique formation that has withstood the power of running water for thousands of years. While the falls can be viewed year-round, they are most impressive in late June and early July during runoff, when the Kickinghorse is at its peak.

10. Hamilton Falls

LOCATION: Yoho National Park
DRIVING DIFFICULTY: Easy
HIKING DIFFICULTY: Easy
HIKING DISTANCE: 700 m
HIKING TIME: 15 min.

It is easy to get sucked into elbowing your way around the shoreline at Emerald Lake and firing off a thousand photos of the picturesque Emerald Lake Lodge. But your blood pressure would benefit more by taking the less used Hamilton Lake trail just a few hundred metres away from the throngs of people, and seeking out the pretty Hamilton Falls instead.

Driving directions

From Field, drive west on the Trans-Canada for 1.5 km to the signed Emerald Lake Road. Continue for 9.0 km to the Emerald Lake parking area at the end of the road. Park where you can. It is best to get there early in the day, especially on weekends, as this place fills up fast and furiously. If you arrive later in the morning or in the afternoon, you might end up parking up to 2 km down the road from the main lot.

Hiking directions

Hamilton Falls is a welcome refuge from the maddening crowds of people milling around Emerald Lake. Note that the trail does not leave from the main kiosk at the lakeshore and so goes undetected by most visitors. At the south end of the main parking area, a brown Parks Canada sign marks the trail for Hamilton Falls and Hamilton Lake. Follow this for 700 m to a small waterfall that is just visible from the trail. Much of the cascade is obscured from sight but comes into view if you drop down from the trail to the edge of the creek.

More to explore

While Emerald Lake and the lodge itself are the obvious attractions for most people, the hike past the falls to Hamilton Lake is a far quieter outing and worth the effort if you have the time. It is 6 km one way, and the trail gains a strenuous 840 m to this secluded alpine lake. On the other hand, Emerald Lake remains one of the Canadian

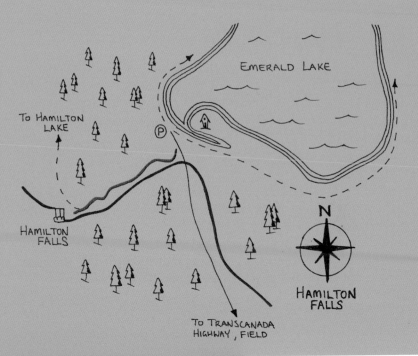

EMERALD LAKE

To HAMILTON
LAKE

HAMILTON
FALLS

N

HAMILTON
FALLS

To TRANSCANADA
HIGHWAY, FIELD

Rockies' classic views, if you're okay taking it in shoulder to shoulder with others around the busy lakeshore trail.

11. Wapta Falls

LOCATION: Yoho National Park
DRIVING DIFFICULTY: Moderate
HIKING DIFFICULTY: Easy
HIKING DISTANCE: 2.4 km
HIKING TIME: 45–60 min.

Wapta Falls is HUGE! Here you will witness the full force of the Kickinghorse River as its entire volume vaults over a wall 30 m high and 150 m wide. This waterfall is one of the largest in the country by volume, a fact that will become obvious from the moment you first see it. While you can expect your clothing to be drenched by the spray from it, the views are well worth the soaking at any time of the year!

Driving directions

From Field, drive west on the Trans-Canada for 25 km. There is no signed trailhead for westbound traffic, as there is no turning lane. Continue for a couple more kilometres to the Yoho National Park boundary, turn around and drive back east to the signed turnoff on your right. Follow the rough gravel road for 1.8 km to a signed trailhead with biffies. This is one of the most popular and easily accessible trails off the Trans-Canada. It is recommended to get there by mid-morning or early evening, especially during the summer.

Alternatively, a viewpoint of the falls from the other side of the river can be accessed via the Beaverfoot Forestry Service Road and the Wapta Falls Recreation Site, which is located at the 7 km mark of the forestry road.

Hiking directions

Follow the wide, well-used trail through forest to a fenced overlook above the Kickinghorse River. The falls won't be visible just yet, but you'll hear the roar from below. From the first viewpoint, the trail begins to descend, with various forks that all end down at the riverbank. From here you can scramble up a rocky mound for a front-row seat to the 30-metre-high waterfall. Expect to get wet as the spray from Wapta Falls is unbelievable, even late in the summer. The falls are accessible year-round, except maybe after a large snowfall.

12. Hospital Creek Falls

LOCATION: Golden
DRIVING DIFFICULTY: Easy
HIKING DIFFICULTY: Easy (depending on depth of creek)
HIKING DISTANCE: 800 m
HIKING TIME: 30 min.

While the short hike to Hospital Creek Falls is certainly not stroller friendly, you just might find one along the way. Need a short hike to stretch your legs or maybe some parts for your car? You've come to the right place. If you can ignore all the trash along the creek, the trail to the falls actually is quite nice. The waterfall itself is a true hidden gem!

Driving directions

From the intersection of the Trans-Canada and Highway 95 in Golden, drive west a few hundred metres on the Trans-Canada through the service strip. At the Ramada Hotel, turn right, onto 12th Street North. Drive into the mobile-home park. Stay left at the fork and follow to the end of the road, which has a large turnaround and unsigned gravel parking area.

Hiking directions

From the parking area, the unmarked trail starts at concrete blocks and initially follows the right-hand side of the creek. After a few hundred metres you'll be forced to cross the creek. At low water the crossing can be made on rocks or logs, but it is best to bring a pair of good sandals and simply expect to get your feet wet on this one.

A short time later a rocky outcrop blocks your passage and you'll have to cross the creek again, and then again, and then one final time before reaching the base of the falls. Best to save this hike for later in the summer, as the creek will be very difficult and dangerous to cross during runoff or after a big rain. The secluded falls are tucked away at the back of the canyon along Hospital Creek.

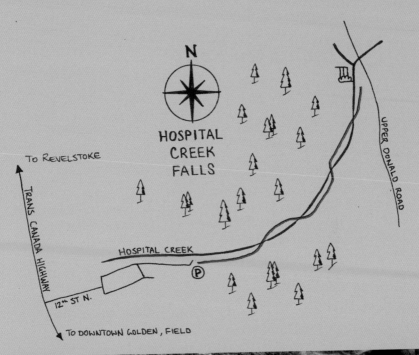

N

HOSPITAL
CREEK
FALLS

To Revelstoke

TRANS CANADA HIGHWAY

HOSPITAL CREEK

ⓅP

12ᵗʰ ST N.

To DOWNTOWN GOLDEN, FIELD

UPPER DONALD ROAD

13. Thompson Falls

LOCATION: Golden
DRIVING DIFFICULTY: Moderate
HIKING DIFFICULTY: Easy
HIKING DISTANCE: 700 m
HIKING TIME: 10 min.

Thompson Falls is a sudden, narrow drop in the Blaeberry River. Consider the size and volume of the water just upstream of the falls and how narrow a slot it drops through. During runoff the river becomes so swollen that the falls are almost entirely submerged.

Driving directions

From Golden, drive west on the Trans-Canada Highway for about 11 km and turn right onto Moberly Branch Road. Go 2.0 km up the hill to a T-intersection and turn left onto Golden Donald Upper Road. After 1.0 km trend right onto Oberg Johnson Road and continue for 1.8 km to another T. A large Recreation Sites and Trails BC sign will be visible across the intersection. Turn left here and reset your trip odometer.

At 0.5 km stay right as the road becomes Blaeberry Road. At 7.2 km stay right again. At 12.5 km there is an unmarked spur road that drops off to the left. Park on the shoulder of the main road and walk the 200 m down to the parking area, or, if you have a higher-clearance vehicle, drive down.

Hiking directions

From the lower parking area, continue for 500 m along the dirt road. With a high-clearance vehicle it is possible to drive this to its end. From here the falls are just through the trees and are visible from a rocky outcrop above the small, narrow gorge.

Alternatively, Thompson Falls can be reached by hiking from the camping area you passed previously on Blaeberry Road. From here the 6 km trail follows alongside the vermilion waters of the river, ending at the falls. It is about 2–2½ hours each way if you choose this option.

N

THOMPSON
FALLS

4×4

BLAEBERRY RIVER

BLAEBERRY RIVER FORESTRY SERVICE ROAD

THOMPSON FALLS
TRAIL – ALTERNATE

TO TRANSCANADA HIGHWAY,
GOLDEN

More to explore

Near the first parking area, a trail drops down onto the slabby riverbed where the Blaeberry River is squeezed through a narrow channel, in some places no more than a metre wide. Take care here, as the rocks are very polished and slippery as seen in the photo.

14. Mummery Glacier Falls

LOCATION: Golden
DRIVING DIFFICULTY: Moderate
HIKING DIFFICULTY: Easy (to viewpoint)
HIKING DISTANCE: 2.5 km
HIKING TIME: 1 hr.

Some things are worth a little extra effort, like chewing your food. Mummery Glacier is a hike that gets better and better the more you chew. Sure, you can hike to the viewpoint at the gravel flats, but what if you decide to finish your meal there? Why not chew your way up the moraine and watch these waterfalls go down nice and easy?

Driving directions

From Golden, drive west on the Trans-Canada for about 11 km and turn right onto Moberly Branch Road. Go 2.0 km up the hill to a T-intersection and turn left onto Golden Donald Upper Road. After 1.0 km trend right, onto Oberg Johnson Road and continue for 1.8 km to another T. A large Recreation Sites and Trails BC sign will be visible across the intersection. Turn left here and reset your trip odometer.

At 0.5 km stay right as the road becomes Blaeberry Road. At 7.2 km and 17.3 km stay right again. At 22.4 km cross the bridge over the Blaeberry River. At 38.8 km cross a bridge over Mummery Creek. At 40.0 km there is an old logging road on the left, typically marked with plenty of flagging tape. Park out of the way, off to the side of either the spur road or the main forestry road. With a high-clearance vehicle it is possible to drive up the old logging road for an additional kilometre, but it is quite steep and occasionally rough with loose rock.

Hiking directions

From the junction of the main forestry road and the old logging road, hike up the old logging road for 1 km to the second parking area. A brown pole marks the trail where it enters the forest and weaves up, down and around large trees for about 1.5 km. The trail exits the trees as it approaches a creek full of large boulders where remnants of a small suspension bridge atop the rocks can be seen. With the bridge out, crossing here is no longer possible. It is best to continue

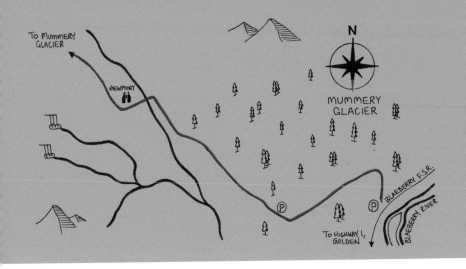

upstream from this point and pick a spot to cross using logs or rocks. Note the location where you have crossed. Once past the creek, enter onto a rocky, gravel flat with views of numerous waterfalls pouring over a massive headwall below the Mummery Glacier. Most folks will take in the views from this point, as the trail becomes indistinct among the rocks and is marked with only intermittent cairns.

More to explore

From the viewpoint, pick up cairns on the far side of the rocky outwash where the trail can be found re-entering the trees. The route then ascends a moraine with close-up views of the waterfalls before delivering you to the top of the headwall and the toe of Mummery Glacier. It is a steep ascent, gaining about 700 m over 2.5 km from the viewpoint on the rocky flats to the toe of the glacier. Allow for an additional two hours each way for this spectacular addition to the hike. It is well worth every effort!

15. Bear Creek Falls

LOCATION: Glacier National Park
DRIVING DIFFICULTY: Easy
HIKING DIFFICULTY: Easy
HIKING DISTANCE: 1.0 km
HIKING TIME: 20 min.

Bear Creek Falls is a popular reprieve from the hustle and bustle of British Columbia's busiest motorway. Escape the buzz of trucks, RVs and the wide selection of commuter vehicles by ducking off the pavement and into this forested refuge. While it is only a short distance to the falls, it feels much farther removed from the highway than that.

Driving directions

Note: Bear Creek Falls is accessible only to eastbound traffic on the Trans-Canada.

From the visitor centre near the summit of Rogers Pass, drive east on the Trans-Canada for about 9 km. Turn right at the signed exit and follow the road to the parking area.

Hiking directions

From the signed trailhead, the route is a continuous and moderate descent before levelling out at the creek. Connaught Creek and Bear Creek Falls can be heard thundering through the canyon from this point. Round the corner to the right, then walk up and over a set of stairs to a misty view near the base of a large waterfall. Good luck keeping yourself and your camera dry.

TO GOLDEN

TRANSCANADA HIGHWAY

CONNAUGHT CREEK

BEAVER RIVER

P

BEAR CREEK FALLS

N

BEAR CREEK FALLS

TO REVELSTOKE

16. Illecillewaet Glacier Falls

LOCATION: Glacier National Park
DRIVING DIFFICULTY: Easy
HIKING DIFFICULTY: Moderate
HIKING DISTANCE: 4.0 km
HIKING TIME: 2 hr.

Driving directions

From the Rogers Pass visitor centre, drive west on the Trans-Canada Highway for about 3 km to the Illecillewaet campground. You might have to drive another kilometre farther to the Loop Brook trailhead, turn around in the pullout and then head back east to access the Illecillewaet and Asulkan Valley trails (the turning lane for westbound traffic was closed in 2019 due to road construction). Park in the day use or hikers parking areas.

If heading towards Rogers Pass from Revelstoke (eastbound traffic), simply follow signs and turn right into the Illecillewaet campground.

Hiking directions

From the trailhead kiosk, follow the well-signed trail system for the Great Glacier trail. The first 2.5 km is relatively flat before the trail steepens as it approaches the waterfall. This massive cascade drains Vaux Glacier and the Illecillewaet Icefield. The elevation gain is more than 400 m, most of it in the last 1.5 km.

Know before you go

Rogers Pass is known as the birthplace of Canadian alpinism. It is easy to see why while hiking around the Illecillewaet and Asulkan Valley trails, with the lofty peaks of Glacier National Park and the Selkirk Mountains towering above. Mount Sir Donald is one of the most recognizable peaks in the country and the tallest in the basin that rings the Illecillewaet Glacier.

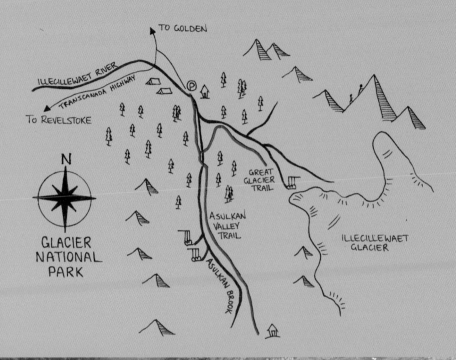

TO GOLDEN

ILLECILLEWAET RIVER

TRANSCANADA HIGHWAY

To REVELSTOKE

GREAT
GLACIER
TRAIL

ASULKAN VALLEY TRAIL

ASULKAN BROOK

ILLECILLEWAET GLACIER

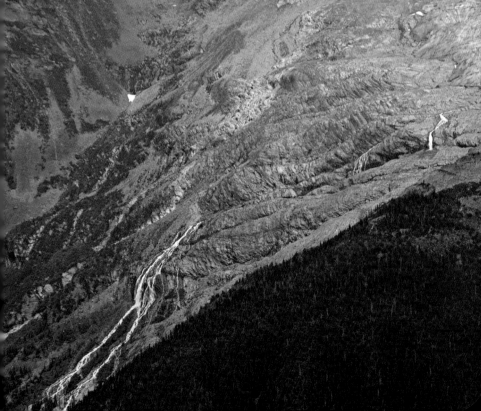

17. Asulkan Valley Waterfalls

LOCATION: Glacier National Park
DRIVING DIFFICULTY: Easy
HIKING DIFFICULTY: Moderate
HIKING DISTANCE: 7.0 km
HIKING TIME: 3 hr.

Being a waterfall in Glacier National Park is like being an aspiring actor in Hollywood: falls are everywhere and only the most famous have recognizable names. The Asulkan Valley trail passes two impressive waterfalls draining small glaciers below The Rampart and The Dome, peaks along Asulkan Ridge which tower high above the valley floor. Under any other circumstances, these waterfalls would be worthy destinations on their own. Unfortunately for the waterfalls, they are only B-list stars compared to other massive vistas in the park.

Driving directions

From the Rogers Pass visitor centre, drive west on the Trans-Canada Highway for about 3 km to the Illecillewaet campground. You might have to go another kilometre farther to the Loop Brook trailhead, turn around in the pullout and then head back east to access the Illecillewaet and Asulkan Valley trails (the turning lane for westbound traffic was closed in 2019 due to road construction). Park in the day use or hikers parking areas.

If heading towards Rogers Pass from Revelstoke (eastbound traffic) simply follow signs and turn right into the Illecillewaet campground.

Hiking directions

From the trailhead kiosk, follow signage and trail markers for the Asulkan Valley. The trail starts by passing the ruins of Glacier House. A pause to read the interpretive signs about the rise and fall of this historic hotel is worth the time. The first 4 km is quite mellow, following alongside the Asulkan Brook. Visible through breaks in the trees around the 3 km mark are two huge cascades pouring down a treed headwall under the Rampart.

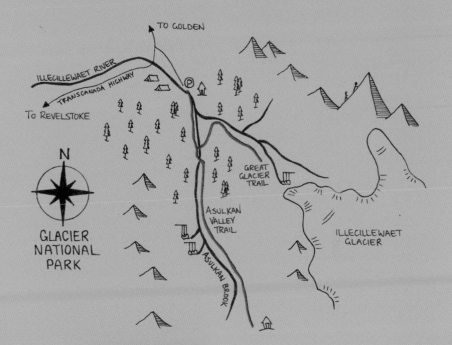

More to explore

After 4 km the trail shows its teeth and starts to climb, gaining moderate elevation at first and then, after crossing a bridge at about 5.3 km, steepening significantly as it ascends a moraine. The Asulkan Cabin marks the end of the trail. Reservations to this backcountry cabin are required and can be made through the Alpine Club of Canada.

18. Akolkolex Falls (Upper)

LOCATION: Revelstoke
DRIVING DIFFICULTY: Moderate
HIKING DIFFICULTY: Easy
HIKING DISTANCE: 500 m
HIKING TIME: 10 min.

The source of Akolkolex River is high on the Albert Icefield, more than 30 km from where the Akolkolex eventually flows into the Columbia River southeast of Revelstoke. However, it is the last kilometre that makes this river truly spectacular as it cartwheels out of the Selkirk Mountains in a series of large cascades to its final destination. There is a lot to see and do in Revelstoke but a trip to Akolkolex Falls is definitely a highlight!

Driving directions

From downtown Revelstoke, head south on Airport Way. From the intersection of Airport Way and Nichol Road, drive south on Airport Way for 14.8 km. Turn left onto the Akolkolex Forestry Service Road (signed). Reset your trip odometer. At 12.5 km turn right onto the Crawford Forestry Service Road. At 18.0 km look for an unmarked pullout with barricades (decommissioned road) on the right-hand side. Park here. If you end up crossing the bridge over the Akolkolex, you've gone too far.

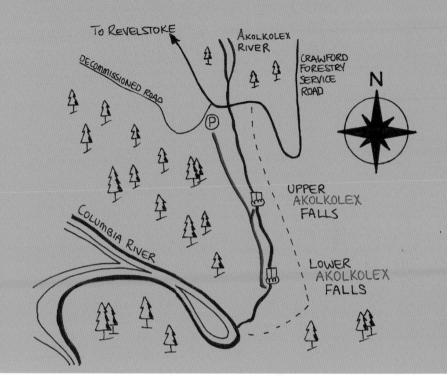

Hiking directions

From the barricades, head towards the Akolkolex River through a thinly forested area. The ground is packed down in the vicinity of the parking lot and develops into a trail as it approaches the river. A fenced viewpoint overlooks the waterfall from above, but if you continue on the main trail, a boot-beaten spur branches off and descends moderately back towards the creek. Crawl over a few downed trees and push through a couple of bushes to a great vantage point near the base of the falls.

The Name Game

Some historical photos from the early 1900s refer to the Upper Akolkolex Falls as "Frayne Falls," but there are no modern references to the waterfall by this name. There are numerous steps on the Akolkolex River besides the two larger falls highlighted in this guide. Some of the other cascades farther downstream are also referred to as Lower Akolkolex Falls by other sources. So, forgive me if I have botched the identification of these waterfalls.

19. Akolkolex Falls (Lower)

LOCATION: Revelstoke
DRIVING DIFFICULTY: Moderate
HIKING DIFFICULTY: Easy
HIKING DISTANCE: 750 m
HIKING TIME: 15 min.

To stop after seeing the upper waterfall would be like going to split firewood with only a hatchet: you will be mad at yourself for making such a silly decision and sorely disappointed when you realize you could have done better. Instead, do yourself a favour and carry on down the trail to the arguably more spectacular lower cascade on the Akolkolex River.

Driving directions

From downtown Revelstoke, head south on Airport Way. From the intersection of Airport Way and Nichol Road, drive south on Airport Way for 14.8 km. Turn left onto the Akolkolex Forestry Service Road (signed). Reset your trip odometer. At 12.5 km turn right, onto the Crawford Forestry Service Road. At 18.0 km look for an unmarked pullout with barricades (decommissioned road) on the right-hand side. Park here. If you end up crossing the bridge over the Akolkolex, you've gone too far.

Hiking directions

From the barricades, head through a thin forest towards the river. The ground is packed down in the vicinity of the parking area and develops into a trail as you approach the river. Head past the overlook for the upper falls and continue down the main trail, losing elevation until you come to a small, exposed viewpoint of the lower falls. Step with extreme caution atop this rocky knob; there isn't much room and there's only air beneath you. Here the Akolkolex River continues its chaotic journey towards the Columbia.

More to explore

Don't stop at the lower falls either. Continue down the trail towards the Columbia River and see even more small cascades along the

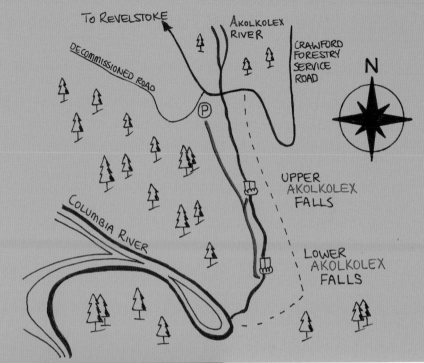

Akolkolex before it makes its final leap into the Columbia. Note that the trail below the Lower Falls lookout becomes quite steep. Alternatively, you can go back to your vehicle, cross the bridge and follow a utility road on foot on the opposite side of the Akolkolex for different vantage points of the various waterfalls.

20. Jordan River Falls

LOCATION: Revelstoke
DRIVING DIFFICULTY: Easy
HIKING DIFFICULTY: Easy
HIKING DISTANCE: 1.3 km
HIKING TIME: 30 min.

Jordan River Falls may be the least known of the Revelstoke waterfall hikes. While it doesn't have a big drop like some of the others nearby such as the Akolkolex, Sutherland or Begbie falls, the hike does have a secluded feel for one so close to town. Although the river is better known for whitewater kayaking and is a popular run for experienced paddlers, it is a peaceful and beautiful hike along the Jordan River to this small waterfall where the hike is as much of a reward as the destination.

Driving directions

In Revelstoke, from the west end of the bridge that crosses the Columbia River, turn right (if driving westbound) onto Westside Road. Drive the paved road for 3.9 km to the Jordan River Forestry Service Road, which is on the left-hand side at the Revelstoke Snowmobile Club staging area. Drive a good gravel road for another 700 m and park on the shoulder just before the bridge. Make sure your vehicle is well off to the side, as the road is quite busy.

Hiking directions

Pick up a trail on the right-hand side of the road just before the bridge. The trail follows the river briefly before it switches back up and over a steep knob. Approximately 300 m from the trailhead, there is a faint Y in the trail. Stay left here, crest a small hill and then descend back to the bank of the river. After another few hundred metres, the trail rises steeply again before dropping down to a boulder-strewn bank near the falls. Young children may need a hand near the boulders and on steeper sections of the trail.

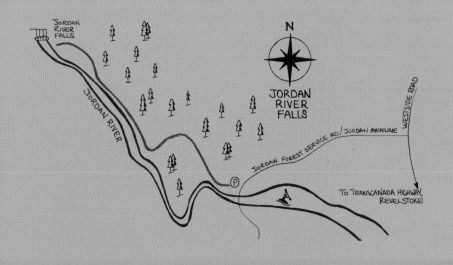

JORDAN
RIVER
FALLS

JORDAN RIVER FALLS

JORDAN RIVER

JORDAN FOREST SERVICE RD / JORDAN MAINLINE

WESTSIDE ROAD

TO TRANSCANADA HIGHWAY, REVELSTOKE

21. Moses Creek Falls

LOCATION: Revelstoke
DRIVING DIFFICULTY: Easy
HIKING DIFFICULTY: Easy
HIKING DISTANCE: 500 m
HIKING TIME: 10 min.

Opinion piece: Moses Creek Falls is one of the most picturesque waterfalls I have ever seen. That is all.

Driving directions

In Revelstoke, from the west side of the bridge that crosses the Columbia River, turn right (if driving westbound) onto Westside Road. Drive the paved road for 6 km to a gravel parking area on your right.

Hiking directions

Pick up a well-used trail at the back of the parking area. The trail cuts down through the grass and across a gravel road before entering the trees. It is only a minute to the upper waterfall but don't stop there. The steep, muddy trail descends alongside as the creek tumbles through a forested, fairytale-like scene to a second beautiful cascade.

Another option is to drive just past the parking area on Westside Road, hang a sharp right and drive down the steep gravel road to a parking area near the Columbia River. From this lower parking lot you can hike uphill to the waterfalls.

For a rainy day

Let's face it, the sun doesn't shine every day. If you find yourself looking for a good rainy-day activity, check out the Revelstoke Dam, which is just upstream of Moses Creek Falls on the Columbia. The visitor centre is open from mid-May to the Labour Day long weekend in September and offers guided and self-guided tours of the facility. To visit the dam, return to Revelstoke and drive 5 km north on Highway 23.

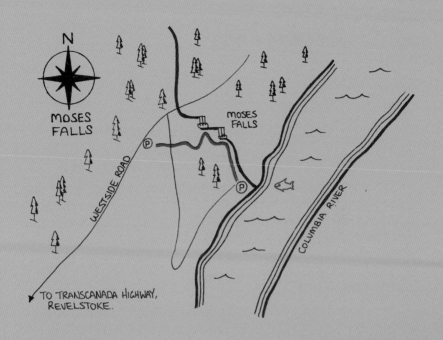

N

MOSES
FALLS

WESTSIDE ROAD

Ⓟ

MOSES
FALLS

Ⓟ

COLUMBIA RIVER

TO TRANSCANADA HIGHWAY,
REVELSTOKE.

22. Begbie Falls

LOCATION: Revelstoke
DRIVING DIFFICULTY: Easy
HIKING DIFFICULTY: Easy
HIKING DISTANCE: 2.3 km
HIKING TIME: 1 hr.

Begbie Falls is likely the best-known and most popular of the cascades in the Revelstoke area. A day can be made exploring the area, as access to the falls is part of the much larger Begbie Creek trail system. Please note this is a shared-use trail network. Be aware of other users, especially mountain bikers.

Driving directions

In Revelstoke, from the west end of the bridge over the Columbia River, turn left (if driving westbound) onto Highway 23 southbound. Continue for 9.1 km and turn left into a parking area signed for Begbie Creek.

Hiking directions

Note: Directions to Begbie Falls are given for access via Bluff Trail.

From parking, follow the well-marked and well-signed Bluff Trail to Begbie Falls. The trail steadily loses elevation as it passes the Begbie Bluffs rock-climbing area and eventually reaches a second parking lot marked for the Begbie Falls recreation site. Continue descending from this parking area and, as the trail begins to flatten out, cut back to the right to a viewing platform near the base of the falls.

Alternative access: 7 km south of the junction of the Trans-Canada and Highway 23, turn left onto Clough Road. Take a right onto Begbie Road and then another right onto the Begbie Falls Forestry Service Road. Park at the signed carpark for the Begbie Falls recreation site. The falls are 300 m, about five minutes, from this parking area.

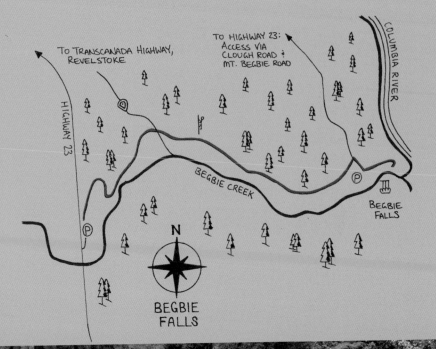

To TRANSCANADA HIGHWAY,
REVELSTOKE

To HIGHWAY 23:
ACCESS VIA
CLOUGH ROAD &
MT. BEGBIE ROAD

COLUMBIA RIVER

HIGHWAY 23

BEGBIE CREEK

BEGBIE
FALLS

N

BEGBIE
FALLS

23. Sutherland Falls

LOCATION: Blanket Creek Provincial Park, Revelstoke
DRIVING DIFFICULTY: Easy
HIKING DIFFICULTY: Easy
HIKING DISTANCE: 150 m
HIKING TIME: 5 min.

If you are so drained of energy from exploring waterfalls that all you can manage is crawling, you can probably still make it to Sutherland Falls. This is one of the shortest "hikes" in the book but it leads to one of the most spectacular waterfalls. Blanket Creek is fed from Blanket Glacier high up in the Monashee Mountains and provides the fuel that enables Sutherland Falls to gush all year long.

Driving directions

In Revelstoke, from the west end of the bridge over the Columbia River, turn left (if driving westbound) onto Highway 23 southbound. Continue for 23.5 km and turn left onto a road signed for Blanket Creek Provincial Park. Follow the winding road downhill for 1.5 km and turn left at another road signed for Sutherland Falls. Park at the signed trailhead.

Hiking directions

Follow the huge, obvious trail for just a few hundred metres to a fenced viewing platform. The trail is stroller friendly. It is possible to get a close-up view of the falls by scrambling up boot-beaten trails beyond the viewing platform.

Notes of Interest

Sutherland Falls is a popular spot to hurl oneself over in a kayak; so says the signage near the viewpoint. In case the warning needs further elaboration, dropping the waterfall in a small plastic boat is dangerous and should be left to expert whitewater kayakers rather than aspiring adrenalin junkies.

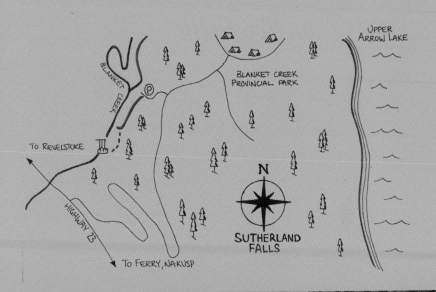

UPPER ARROW LAKE

BLANKET CREEK

BLANKET CREEK PROVINCIAL PARK

TO REVELSTOKE

HIGHWAY 23

TO FERRY, NAKUSP

N

SUTHERLAND FALLS

24. Pingston Falls

LOCATION: Revelstoke
DRIVING DIFFICULTY: Moderate
HIKING DIFFICULTY: Easy
HIKING DISTANCE: 200 m
HIKING TIME: 5 min.

It is a long drive to Pingston Falls down a very mediocre forestry road, so if your objective is the waterfall itself, you could be a little disappointed by the time and effort required. However, combined with a beach camp near the lake and some paddling around the shoreline, this is a spot where a mediocre outing can fast become an outstanding one. Enjoy this secluded little chunk of paradise!

Driving directions

From Revelstoke, drive 48 km south on Highway 23 to the Shelter Bay Forestry Service Road and turn right. Reset your trip odometer. The gravel road is generally in good shape and sees a fair bit of traffic. There are a number of tempting intersecting logging roads and spurs, but ignore them all and stay on the main forestry road. With that in mind, follow directions at these waypoints:

- Right at 2.3 km
- Right at 3.0 km
- Left at 12.4 km
- Left at 16.7 km
- Left at 22.3 km
- Left at 25.0 km

At the 25 km mark, a much rougher road descends for 1 km to the lakeshore, passing an old cabin on the right. Turn around where possible and park at the end of the road.

Hiking directions

From the end of the road, pick up faint trails leading into the trees, trending south. These trails merge and head towards a small inlet out of sight on the lakeshore. As you follow the high banks above the shore, Pingston Falls becomes visible as it drains Pingston Creek into Upper Arrow Lake.

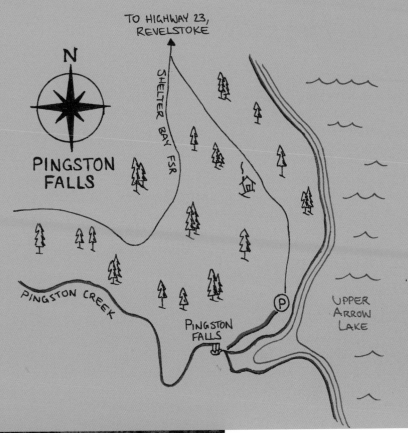

Know before you go

The beach on Arrow Lake may be one of the premier spots described in this book to spend a night, and it won't cost a dime. Unless, that is, you get your vehicle stuck in the sand and need an extraction, which would be very expensive. Consider yourself warned: don't drive onto the beach!

25. Frog Falls

LOCATION: Revelstoke
DRIVING DIFFICULTY: Moderate
HIKING DIFFICULTY: Easy
HIKING DISTANCE: 100 m
HIKING TIME: <5 min.

Frog Falls is an easy one to disregard given the many other waterfalls in the Revelstoke area that are closer to highways and don't involve travel on a forestry road. Nonetheless, this is a big, beautiful waterfall with a forestry recreation site nearby (read: free camping!). Take extra care when driving on the Wap–Mabel Lake FSR, though, as it is an active haul road.

Driving directions

From Revelstoke, at the junction of the Trans-Canada Highway and Highway 23, drive west on the Trans-Canada for 23 km and turn left onto the Wap–Mabel Lake Forestry Service Road. Reset your trip odometer. Cross bridges at 1.5 km, 3.4 km and 4.5 km. Turn left at 4.6 km onto a secondary logging road (unsigned). Drive 700 m and turn left onto a signed decommissioned road. Drive another 300 m and turn left onto a small spur which dead-ends after another 100 m. Turn around where possible and park.

Hiking directions

Frog Falls is out of sight but can be heard from here. From the end of the small branch road, hike left into the trees to a nearby viewpoint atop the bouldery clifftop. This is the best view of the falls. Notice some fenced infrastructure perched atop the impressive waterfall.

Alternative access

A second viewpoint is directly above the waterfall and can be accessed by turning left up a spur road just before the Frog Falls Recreation Site. Park near a hydroelectric unit a short distance up this road and hike about 200 m to the overlook at the top of the falls.

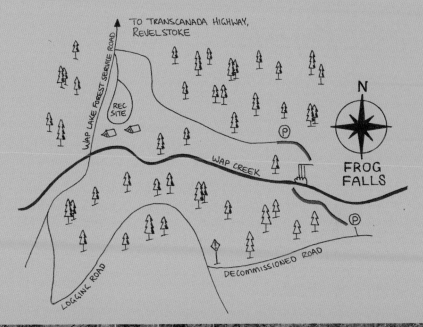

TO TRANSCANADA HIGHWAY,
REVELSTOKE

WAP LAKE FOREST SERVICE ROAD

REC SITE

N

WAP CREEK

Ⓟ

FROG
FALLS

Ⓟ

LOGGING ROAD

DECOMMISSIONED ROAD

26. Kay Falls

LOCATION: Craigellachie
DRIVING DIFFICULTY: Easy
HIKING DIFFICULTY: Easy
HIKING DISTANCE: 200 m
HIKING TIME: 5 min.

Kay Falls is a gem of a waterfall hidden from sight just off the Trans-Canada Highway. Most commuters blow right by it without a thought, completely unaware of its existence. The cataract itself is deceptively tall amid the dense cedar forest and is well worth what little effort it takes to reach it.

Driving directions

From the junction of the Trans-Canada and Highway 23 in Revelstoke, drive west on the Trans-Canada for 35 km. The pullout is on the right just before the Kay Creek bridge, or if driving eastbound, pull out on the left just after the bridge. It is advisable to use the

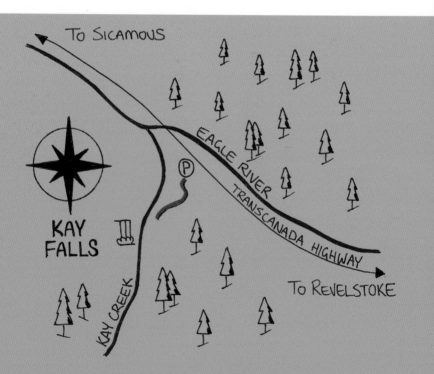

eastbound pullout so as to avoid accidentally involving yourself in a game of chicken on one of the busiest highways in western Canada.

Hiking directions

An unmarked but well-used trail leaves the eastbound pullout and heads into the trees. A short uphill stroll leads to the base of a spectacular waterfall hidden just out of view from the highway. It is accessible year-round and is one of the most beautiful cascades in this guidebook.

27. Crazy Creek Falls

LOCATION: Craigellachie
DRIVING DIFFICULTY: Easy
HIKING DIFFICULTY: Easy
HIKING DISTANCE: 1.0 km
HIKING TIME: 30 min.

I debated whether to include this hike, as fees are required to use the trails and view the waterfalls. That said, Crazy Creek has spent a substantial amount of money and resources in building an amazing suspension bridge and viewing platforms, as well as on trail development. Plus, it's never a bad day when hot pools are in the equation.

Driving directions

From the junction of the Trans-Canada and Highway 23 in Revelstoke, drive west on the Trans-Canada for 39 km. Turn into one of two signed parking areas for Crazy Creek. The summer parking lot off the westbound lane gives access to the suspension bridge and waterfalls, while the main parking is open year-round with access to the hot springs, trails and suspension bridge.

Hiking directions

From either access point, follow well-used and well-maintained trails to the viewing platforms or the suspension bridge overlooking Crazy Creek Falls. In my opinion, I don't know that it is worth paying to view a waterfall, but the vantage point from the suspension bridge is a fun and unique perspective.

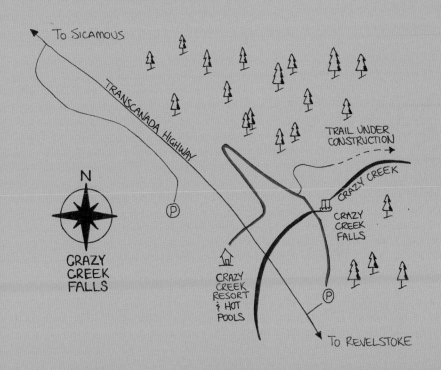

To Sicamous

TRANSCANADA HIGHWAY

N

CRAZY
CREEK
FALLS

TRAIL UNDER
CONSTRUCTION

CRAZY CREEK

CRAZY
CREEK
FALLS

CRAZY
CREEK
RESORT
& HOT
POOLS

To Revelstoke

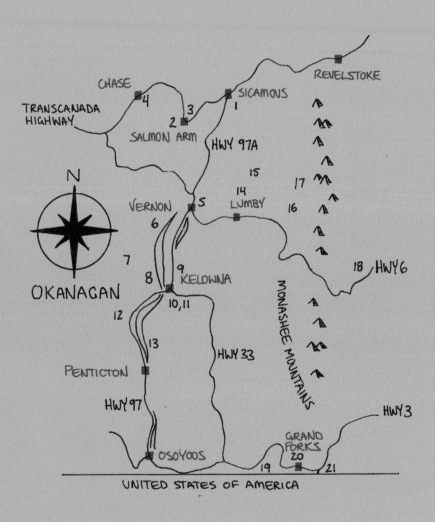

CHAPTER 4

Okanagan & Boundary

In an area known more for wine, lakes, orchards, sun, heat and, well, pretty much everything other than waterfalls, it's a pleasant surprise to find them in relative abundance throughout the Okanagan.

Where the waterfalls of the Rockies, Purcells, Selkirks and Monashees reliably gush year-round with water fed by high glaciers, the cascades of the Okanagan surge for only a few weeks during spring runoff before being reduced to mere trickles later in the summer. If you have come to the area expecting to spend your days restricted to relaxing on beaches or enjoying the tasting rooms of the nearly two hundred wineries, fear not! You can also discover nearly two dozen waterfalls tucked away in the hills of the Okanagan.

The region detailed in this section extends from the Trans-Canada Highway in the north, then south along the Highway 97 corridor to Highway 3, then back eastward to the Arrow Lakes, which divide the Selkirk and Monashee ranges. Major service centres include Sicamous, Salmon Arm and Chase on the Trans-Canada Highway. Towns providing full amenities along the Highway 97 corridor include Vernon, Kelowna, Penticton, Oliver and Osoyoos. If you're driving back east on Highway 3, Midway, Greenwood, Grand Forks and Christina Lake are your options.

1. Sicamous Creek Falls

LOCATION: Sicamous
DRIVING DIFFICULTY: Easy
HIKING DIFFICULTY: Easy
HIKING DISTANCE: 200 m
HIKING TIME: 5 min.

Sicamous Creek Falls is a small and unique waterfall straddling a large boulder that sits squarely in the middle of the creekbed. It's a great spot for a short jaunt as you pass through the Shuswap region, just off the Trans-Canada Highway.

Driving directions

From the junction of the Trans-Canada and Highway 97A in Sicamous, drive 3.6 km south on 97A. Turn left onto Two Mile Road. Drive 400 m up the road to a signed parking area on the right-hand side.

Hiking directions

At the upper end of the parking lot, a trailhead kiosk highlights the various routes in the area. From here the short trail descends gently to a viewpoint near the base of the falls.

Know before you go

The trail network along Sicamous Creek was closed during the 2019 summer season due to two fatalities that year. Please check the current status of the trail before heading to the falls. Trail information is available online from the Shuswap Trail Alliance: shuswaptrails.com/trails.php. This is a good reminder to stay on marked and established trails, as well as behind guardrails and barriers where present.

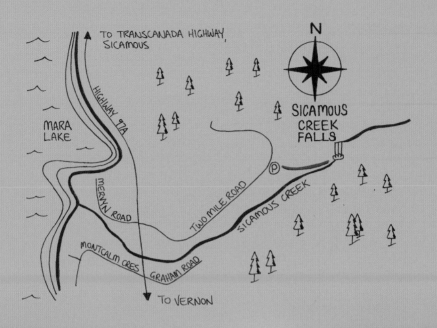

2. Syphon Falls

LOCATION: Salmon Arm
DRIVING DIFFICULTY: Easy
HIKING DIFFICULTY: Easy
HIKING DISTANCE: 650 m
HIKING TIME: 15 min.

Syphon Falls is a tiny cascade tucked away in the hills above the city of Salmon Arm. It's a short hike through a wooded area to this secluded sanctuary. The area around the base of the falls makes a great spot to read a book, have a picnic, even attempt some short rock-climbing routes if you've brought the gear. This is a very cool treasure right in the backyard of Salmon Arm.

Driving directions

From Highway 1 in Salmon Arm, turn left onto 1st Avenue SW in the west end of town. Reset your trip odometer. Drive 3.5 km and turn left onto 30th Avenue NW. At 4.3 km turn right onto 60th Street NW. At 5.4 km turn left into a parking area.

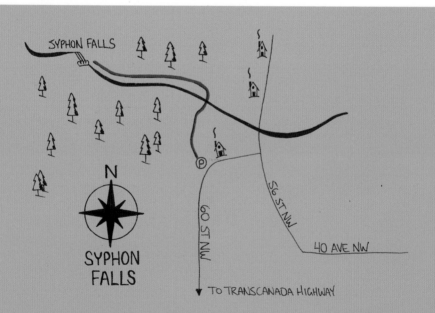

Hiking directions

From the signed trailhead, follow directions for Syphon Falls. The trail passes alongside a couple of residences in a grassy clearing before entering trees and crossing a small stream. Turn left after crossing the stream. The trail then begins to ascend moderately for the next 500 m before arriving at the base of this small, hidden waterfall.

Syphon Falls can be accessed year-round, but they can come close to running dry by the end of the hot summer months or in a very dry year.

3. Margaret Falls

LOCATION: Herald Provincial Park, Salmon Arm
DRIVING DIFFICULTY: Easy
HIKING DIFFICULTY: Easy
HIKING DISTANCE: 500 m
HIKING TIME: 15 min.

If Margaret Falls were in Banff or Jasper national park, the result would be something similar to Johnston Canyon: inundation with tour buses and thousands of people every day. Fortunately, Margaret Falls is not in Banff National Park. It is not even on a major highway, which helps keep the hordes of visitors at bay. Go and discover one of the most beautiful waterfalls in the province for yourself.

Driving directions

From the Trans-Canada Highway in Salmon Arm, drive west and turn right onto Sunnybrae–Canoe Point Road, which is just west of town. Follow this for 11.5 km and turn left into a signed parking area for Margaret Falls.

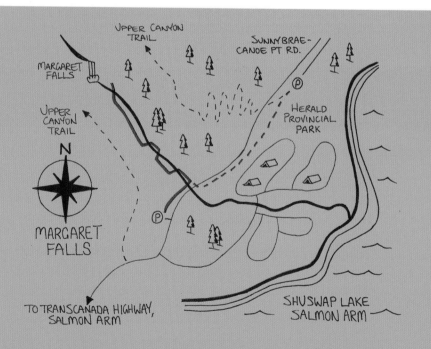

Hiking directions

From the outhouse, follow the brand new trail into a dark canyon, criss-crossing Reineker Creek over several bridges. You'll soon find yourself at a large viewing platform at the base of a spectacular waterfall that is truly out of this world. The trail was wiped out by flooding in 2017 and has been expertly reconstructed since, making it stroller-friendly and accessible year round. Enjoy!

The walk can be extended by parking farther up the road at the Herald Provincial Park day use area and following signed trails back towards the creek.

4. Chase Creek Falls

LOCATION: Chase
DRIVING DIFFICULTY: Easy
HIKING DIFFICULTY: Easy
HIKING DISTANCE: 300 m
HIKING TIME: 10 min.

Speaking from experience and my own self-proclaimed "expertise" in the field, nothing beats having a waterfall right in the neighbourhood. The mountain towns of British Columbia are incredibly fortunate to have such beautiful natural treasures just minutes from our doorsteps.

Driving directions

From the Trans-Canada Highway alongside the town of Chase, turn west onto Coburn Street (right turn if heading westbound through town). Take the next right onto Paquette Road. The road dead-ends

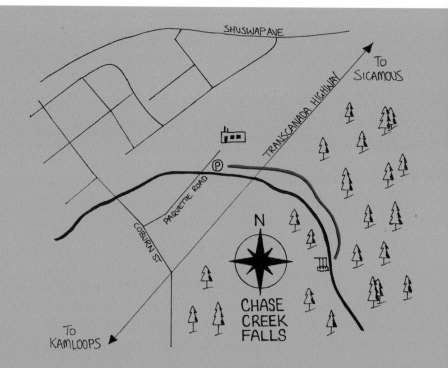

near a fenced maintenance yard where there is a parking area on the right signed for Chase Creek Falls.

Hiking directions

From the parking area, walk under the highway on the gravel path and follow along the left-hand side of the creek for about ten minutes to the base of a small waterfall. The best time to visit is July through October. In years when runoff is especially high the falls might not be accessible until later in the spring, as water can cover the trail on approach.

5. BX Falls

LOCATION: Vernon
DRIVING DIFFICULTY: Easy
HIKING DIFFICULTY: Easy
HIKING DISTANCE: 400 m
HIKING TIME: 15 min.

The BX Creek trails are the perfect escape from the blistering heat of the Okanagan summer. The shady trail follows BX Creek right in the town of Vernon. You can soak your feet, wade in the slower-moving portions of the creek or simply take refuge from the sun on the forested trails.

Driving directions

From Highway 97 in Vernon, turn east onto 48th Avenue, which becomes Silver Star Road. Turn right onto Tillicum Road and follow that for 1 km. Just after a hard right-hand bend in the road, pull into a parking area at the BX Creek trailhead.

Hiking directions

From the signed trailhead, follow the route downstream on the left-hand side of the creek. The creek drops away as the path bends to the left along the back of some houses. As of 2019 a new set of stairs was under construction, offering a direct route down into the canyon which reunites with the creek at the base of BX Falls. A little farther along the main trail, past the junction with the waterfall, you can also descend a steep trail and an older set of stairs to an obscured viewpoint of the falls.

For a longer outing, continue along the BX Creek trail, a 6 km out and back trip from the parking area. The trail is accessible year-round, although snowshoes may be necessary in the wintertime.

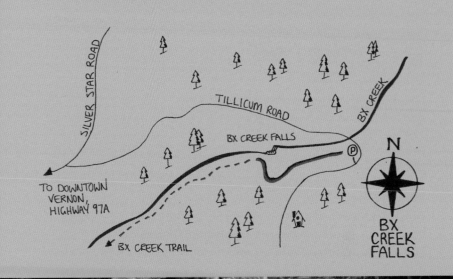

SILVER STAR ROAD

TILLICUM ROAD

BX CREEK

BX CREEK FALLS

TO DOWNTOWN VERNON, HIGHWAY 97A

P

BX CREEK TRAIL

N

BX CREEK FALLS

6. Fintry Falls

LOCATION: Fintry Provincial Park, Kelowna
DRIVING DIFFICULTY: Easy
HIKING DIFFICULTY: Easy
HIKING DISTANCE: 500 m
HIKING TIME: 20 min.

Fintry Provincial Park is the former site of the historic Fintry Estate. which featured a large manor, barns, gardens and a power generation and irrigation system. Today the park boasts camping, beaches, swimming, fishing, paddling, wildlife viewing, hiking and obviously (for our purposes at least) a short hike to a beautiful waterfall!

Driving directions

From Westside Road on the west shore of Okanagan Lake, follow signs for Fintry Provincial Park and turn onto Fintry Delta Road, about 31 km north of the junction with Highway 97. Drive 2 km down the switchbacking road to a junction at the bottom of the hill. Proceed straight ahead, cross the bridge over the creek and park at the signed trailhead on the left.

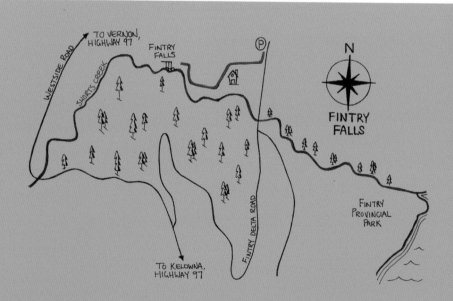

Hiking directions

From the signed trailhead, walk past the old barn and towards the creek before tackling the 396 steps to the viewing platform overlooking the three-tiered Fintry Falls. From the viewpoint you can return the way you came by descending the stairs or continue along the boardwalk to the right, which meets up with a gravel road. The road descends back to the parking area to complete the loop.

7. Christie Falls

LOCATION: Kelowna
DRIVING DIFFICULTY: Difficult (high-clearance vehicle recommended)
HIKING DIFFICULTY: Easy
HIKING DISTANCE: 1.2 km
HIKING TIME: 45 min.

Christie Falls is one of the truly unique places covered in this guidebook. The stream that feeds it barely qualifies as a watercourse, but the view from the base of the falls is simply memorable. The small stream plummets over the edge of a tall, overhanging cliff, and what little water doesn't turn to mist before reaching the ground only dampens the mossy rocks at the foot of the rock wall.

While winter access requires a snowmobile, the waterfall occasionally forms a stunning cone of ice, and it would be well worth the effort to see this wintertime spectacle.

Driving directions

It's a rough road to Christie Falls, but if you have the vehicle to do it, DO IT! This is one of the most distinctive waterfalls in the guidebook and a one of a kind experience. From Westside Road on the west shore of Okanagan Lake, drive past Bear Creek Provincial Park and turn left onto the Bear Lake Forestry Service Road, 8.3 km from the junction with Highway 97. Reset your trip odometer.

At 12.0 km turn right, onto Esperon Forestry Service Road. At 22.0 km stay left. At 22.8 turn right, onto Terrace Mountain Road. At 26.5 km turn left (there is a sign for Christie Falls but it's only visible from the other direction). At 28.7 km park at a widening in the road, or with a high-clearance 4×4 you can drive the extra 200 m to a large turnaround and unmarked parking area.

Hiking directions

From the parking area, follow a trail through the charred remnants of 2003's Terrace Mountain fire. After a few hundred metres cross the small creek and continue along the trail that leads to the edge of the plateau. The trail bends sharply to the left as it descends the

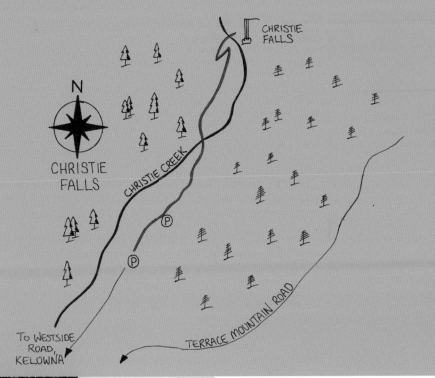

steep slope off the plateau. Use caution! Progress is aided by ropes to the base of the waterfall.

Access is best attempted after mid-June and before mid-October. Any earlier or later and you might find the road blocked by snow. By late summer the waterfall slows to a trickle, mostly just mist. Christie Falls is fast becoming one of the most popular hikes in the Kelowna area. Rock climbers may be found attempting to scale the difficult routes on the wall behind the waterfall. Enjoy!

8. Bear Creek Falls

LOCATION: Bear Creek Provincial Park, Kelowna
DRIVING DIFFICULTY: Easy
HIKING DIFFICULTY: Easy
HIKING DISTANCE: 500 m
HIKING TIME: 15 min. to viewpoint

Although Bear Creek Provincial Park is one of the most popular summer camping destinations in the Kelowna region, don't let that deter you from hiking to one of the most spectacular waterfalls in the Okanagan. The cottonwood-lined creek below the cascade's lookouts offers refuge from the summer sun, a chance to dip your toes and beat the heat.

Driving directions

From Westside Road on the west shore of Okanagan Lake, follow signs for Bear Creek Provincial Park and enter a signed parking area on the left side of the road, 6.7 km north of the junction with Highway 97.

Hiking directions

From the parking area, follow the well-used and well-marked trail. Cross the bridge and ascend stairs to various viewpoints overlooking Bear Creek Falls.

It is possible to get to the base of this fall, which makes a good swimming hole in the heat of the Okanagan summer. Cross the second bridge and pick up a boot-beaten trail on the right. It follows the left-hand side of the creek and then drops into the

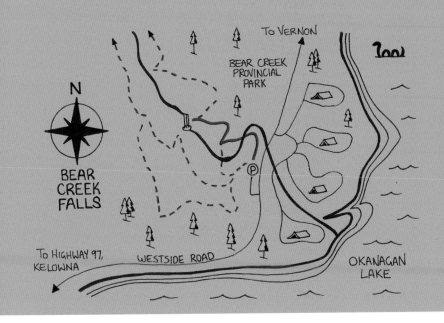

creekbed before crossing back and forth. You will need good foot-wear and low water to get to the base of the falls. In some years this might not even be possible until later in the summer.

Know before you go

The trail system around Bear Creek Provincial Park is quite extensive, offering hikes as short as 15 to 20 minutes and as long as half a day. Mid Canyon Trail is a 1.4 km loop, Canyon Rim Trail a 2.5 km loop. The open slopes face southeast and take sun for most of the day during the summer, so be sure to pack sunscreen, hats and lots of water if you plan to be out exploring for any amount of time. It is recommended to hike early in the day or in the evening to avoid the blistering Okanagan summer sun.

9. Mill Creek Falls

LOCATION: Kelowna
DRIVING DIFFICULTY: Easy
HIKING DIFFICULTY: Easy
HIKING DISTANCE: 700 m
HIKING TIME: 15 min.

Mill Creek Falls is a short and sweet hike to stretch your legs between wine tastings or if you are simply passing through. It is a great spot for little kids and the trail is stroller-friendly.

Driving directions

From Highway 97 through Kelowna, turn onto Old Vernon Road. Follow along to Spencer Road and look for a parking area on your right signed for Mill Creek Regional Park.

Hiking directions

From parking, follow the wide gravel trail along the right-hand side of the creek. Cross the bridge and go to either the base of the falls or slightly farther to a perch atop the falls. The trail is flat and well maintained, making it stroller and kid friendly. Remember to keep dogs leashed and clean up after your fur-babies.

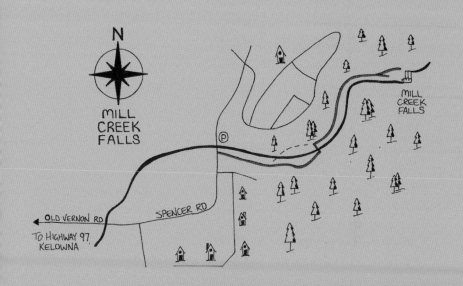

N

MILL
CREEK
FALLS

MILL
CREEK
FALLS

OLD VERNON RD

SPENCER RD

TO HIGHWAY 97
KELOWNA

10. Canyon Falls

LOCATION: Kelowna
DRIVING DIFFICULTY: Easy
HIKING DIFFICULTY: Easy
HIKING DISTANCE: 1 km
HIKING TIME: 20 min.

Everyone loves a deal: two shoes for the price of one, two pant legs for the price of one... How about two waterfalls, some fresh air and exercise for the low, low price of nil? Any takers? The Crawford–Canyon Falls Trail leads you to two waterfalls on the outskirts of the beautiful city of Kelowna. What a deal!

Driving directions

Driving to this trailhead is going to feel like a maze in a puzzle book. An easier method is to grab your phone, search for Crawford Falls Trail and let the robo-voice do the rest. For the purists, here are the directions, from Highway 97 in Kelowna:

- Turn south onto Cooper Road.
- Turn right onto Benvoulin Road.
- Turn right onto Casorso Road.
- Turn left onto Gordon Road.
- Turn left onto DeHart Road.
- Turn right onto Crawford Road.
- Turn right onto Westridge Drive.
- Turn right onto Canyon Ridge Crescent.
- Turn right onto Canyon Falls Court.
- Park on the right-hand side of the road (unmarked).

Hiking directions

From the parking area, follow a trail along the back of the houses. After a few hundred metres turn right at the junction at a fenced overlook and go through the gate. The trail then descends steeply into the canyon. When it flattens out, turn right before descending a set of aluminum stairs to near the base of the first waterfall. This is Canyon Falls.

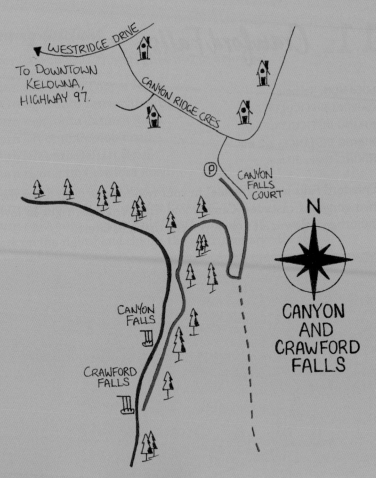

WESTRIDGE DRIVE

TO DOWNTOWN
KELOWNA,
HIGHWAY 97.

CANYON RIDGE CRES

CANYON
FALLS
COURT

N

CANYON
AND
CRAWFORD
FALLS

CANYON
FALLS

CRAWFORD
FALLS

Crawford Falls is a short distance farther, but it involves a delicate scramble up and over a bouldery cliff to the left of the lower fall. Once you're on top it is just a couple of extra minutes to Crawford Falls, the upper and larger of the two cascades.

13. Naramata Falls

LOCATION: Naramata
DRIVING DIFFICULTY: Easy
HIKING DIFFICULTY: Easy
HIKING DISTANCE: 1 km
HIKING TIME: 25 min.

Have you ever felt like you've had too many wine tastings? Yeah, me neither. However, if you do find yourself on the Naramata Bench wondering if there is more to life than delicious wine, you just might find the answer at Naramata Falls. This is a short, shady hike off the wine trail to a little-known waterfall above the vineyards and orchards in the heart of BC's wine country. Next time you find yourself in between tastings, be sure to check this one out.

Driving directions

From Penticton, follow Naramata Road along the east side of Okanagan Lake to an obscure turnoff onto an unnamed road signed for Creek Park. The road ends in a parking area with an outhouse and a signed trailhead.

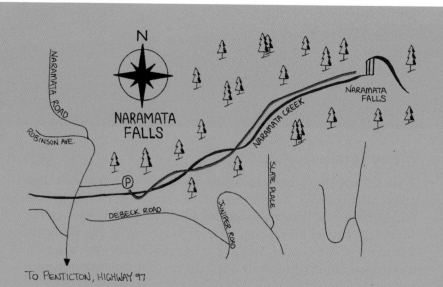

Hiking directions

Follow the trail as it hops from one side of the creek to the other with three bridge and two log/rock crossings. As the trail approaches the waterfall, some lesser used trails fork off to the left but it is best to stay low along the creek. While the stream may wet your feet in the early season, its flow drops off substantially later in the summer.

14. Shuswap Falls

LOCATION: Lumby
DRIVING DIFFICULTY: Easy
HIKING DIFFICULTY: Easy
HIKING DISTANCE: 200 m
HIKING TIME: 5 min.

It is British Columbia's waterways that power our homes, our offices and soon our vehicles. Streams and rivers are forever altered by the presence of hydroelectric generating stations. Here, at the site of the Wilsey Dam, one can see first-hand how we have capitalized on the terrain and water features in this province. The mellow Shuswap River is suddenly choked off at Shuswap Falls, where it thunders through steep, narrow canyons before continuing its journey northward. This feature is perfect to cash in on generating electricity.

Driving directions

From the intersection of Highway 6 and Park Road in Lumby, turn north onto Park Road. After 600 m the street becomes Shuswap Ave. After another kilometre the street becomes the Lumby–Mabel Lake Road. From the intersection in Lumby it is 16.5 km to the BC Hydro Recreation Site overlooking the Wilsey Dam and Shuswap Falls. Turn left into the recreation site and park.

Hiking directions

From parking, follow the broad pathway towards the sound of the river surging just out of sight. A fenced overlook offers an opportunity to peer straight down into the roiling water of the Shuswap River as it pounds through the canyon below.

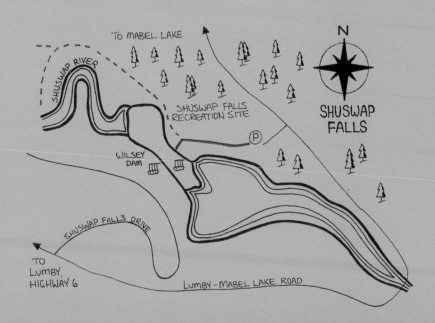

TO MABEL LAKE

SHUSWAP RIVER

N

SHUSWAP FALLS

SHUSWAP FALLS
RECREATION SITE

P

WILSEY
DAM

SHUSWAP FALLS DRIVE

TO
LUMBY,
HIGHWAY 6

LUMBY - MABEL LAKE ROAD

15. Cascade Falls

LOCATION: Lumby
DRIVING DIFFICULTY: Moderate
HIKING DIFFICULTY: Easy
HIKING DISTANCE: 500 m
HIKING TIME: 10 min.

Cascade Falls is the epitome of hidden gems: one of the most stunning waterfalls in the Okanagan, if not the province, tucked away near Mabel Lake. There are no landmarks to signify either the parking area or trailhead, so please take it on faith that we're leading you to the right place. You won't be disappointed in having made the journey to what feels like a much more remote area in BC's interior.

Driving directions

From the intersection of Highway 6 and Park Road in Lumby: turn north onto Park Road. Reset your trip odometer. After 600 m the street becomes Shuswap Ave. After another kilometre the street becomes Lumby–Mabel Lake Road. The pavement ends at 34.7 km. At 43.5 km round a tight left-hand bend in the gravel road just after the 15 km sign and park on the left in an unmarked widening on the road.

Hiking directions

The unmarked trail starts at the sharp bend on the upstream side of the road. The trail ascends on the left side of the creek in a narrow, mossy canyon. As you approach the base of the falls, cross the creek on rocks and fallen logs to the right side of the stream where you will be treated to a front row seat to one of the most beautiful waterfalls in the Okanagan.

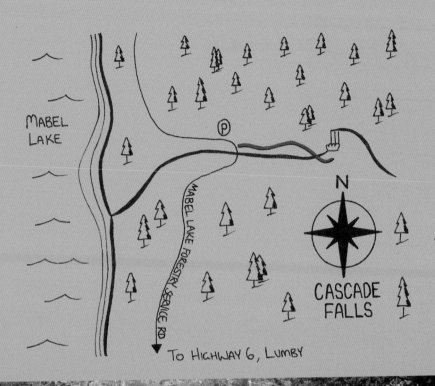

MABEL LAKE

Ⓟ

N

CASCADE
FALLS

MABEL LAKE FORESTRY SERVICE RD.

TO HIGHWAY 6, LUMBY

16. Brenda Falls

LOCATION: Cherryville
DRIVING DIFFICULTY: Easy
HIKING DIFFICULTY: Easy
HIKING DISTANCE: 300 m
HIKING TIME: 5 min.

Similar to the dam at Shuswap Falls, the Sugar Lake Dam capitalizes on a sudden drop in the river to generate electricity. It was put in place to complement the Wilsey Dam farther downstream and was intended to add generating capacity. Brenda Falls is located below the dam, although in the spring the falls become nearly submerged by the high flow from runoff. Later in the summer and in autumn water passing over the dam spillway tumbles down the rocky steps below.

Driving directions

In Cherryville, turn at Frank's General Store and reset your trip odometer. Although the paved road ends at 13.5 km, the gravel road beyond is very well maintained. Turn left onto Reiter Creek Forestry Road at 16.8 km. A small road branches off after 200 m and is gated shortly after. Park before the gate and off to the side so as not to block access to the roadway beyond.

Hiking directions

Walk around the gate and follow the utility road past the dam. Shortly after, pick up a boot-beaten trail on the left which descends steeply to the shoreline below the dam. Brenda Falls is below the Sugar Lake Dam, where the Shuswap River tumbles down a series of rocky outcroppings. Scoping out the dam and falls is a worthwhile stop en route to Rainbow Falls.

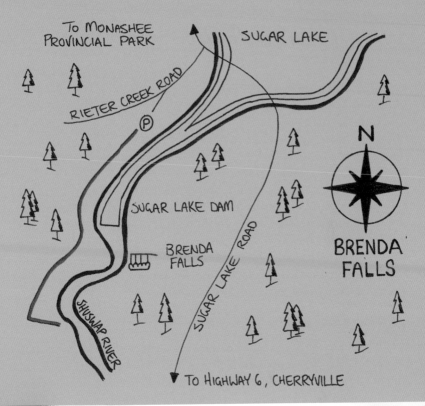

To MONASHEE PROVINCIAL PARK

SUGAR LAKE

RIETER CREEK ROAD

Ⓟ

SUGAR LAKE DAM

BRENDA FALLS

SHUSWAP RIVER

SUGAR LAKE ROAD

N

BRENDA FALLS

To HIGHWAY 6, CHERRYVILLE

17. Rainbow Falls

LOCATION: Monashee Provincial Park, Cherryville
DRIVING DIFFICULTY: Moderate
HIKING DIFFICULTY: Easy
HIKING DISTANCE: 250 m
HIKING TIME: 5 min.

Fuelled by melting snow high in the Monashee Mountains, Rainbow Falls is a stunning and powerful waterfall in the heart of BC's Interior. The mist from the falls carries for hundreds of metres through this remote and forested area along Spectrum Creek. The terrain around Rainbow Falls is a small, stand-alone portion of Monashee Provincial Park; the main boundary is farther north and east, encompassing the alpine lakes and mountains of the Monashees.

Driving directions

In Cherryville, turn at Frank's General Store and reset your trip odometer. The paved road ends at 13.5 km. Follow Sugar Lake Road for 38.1 km and turn right onto Spectrum Creek Forestry Service Road (signed for Monashee Provincial Park). Reset your trip odo again.

Turn right at 1.2 km. Turn left at 4.1 km (signed for Rainbow Falls). Turn right at 4.5 km. Park in the Rainbow Falls parking lot at 4.7 km.

Hiking directions

Trailhead signage is at the far end of the parking lot. Follow a well-used trail as it descends to Spectrum Creek. To get the best view of this enormous waterfall, follow the trail that branches off to the left and climbs briefly to a great vantage overlooking the falls. Expect to get wet: the mist from Rainbow Falls is spectacular.

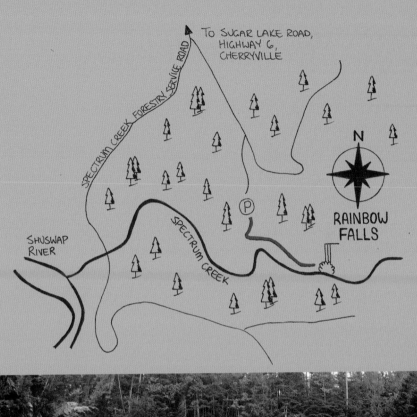

TO SUGAR LAKE ROAD, HIGHWAY 6, CHERRYVILLE

SPECTRUM CREEK FORESTRY SERVICE ROAD

N

RAINBOW FALLS

SHUSWAP RIVER

SPECTRUM CREEK

18. Happy Hippie Hole

LOCATION: Needles
DRIVING DIFFICULTY: Moderate
HIKING DIFFICULTY: Easy
HIKING DISTANCE: 100 m
HIKING TIME: <5 min.

The inclusion of the Hippie Hole in this book is less for the small waterfall that flows into it and more for its being one of the greatest swimming holes in the province. Its relatively remote location keeps the crowds at bay, and while we can't guarantee a hippie sighting at this location, odds are high you won't be alone. Respect other users, and as always, please keep the area clean for the enjoyment of all visitors.

Driving directions

From the Needles Ferry, drive 6 km west on Highway 6 and turn right onto Whatshan Road. Reset your trip odometer. Immediately after turning off the highway, continue past the first left-hand turn and follow signs for Whatshan Lake Retreat. Continue straight at 0.7 km. Stay left at 1.5 km. Shortly after, you will cross a bridge over a small canyon. There are places to park on both sides of the road at either end of the bridge.

Hiking directions

Peer down from the bridge to view the swimming hole and pick your route in from either side. The trail on the left-hand side of the creek hops along rocks to where the creek pools below a tiny waterfall. The trail on the right-hand side stays a little higher and leads to the back of the swimming hole, where a ladder is fastened to the rocky wall that rims the pool. The Hippie Hole is a great place to stay cool and happy in the summer. Play safe!

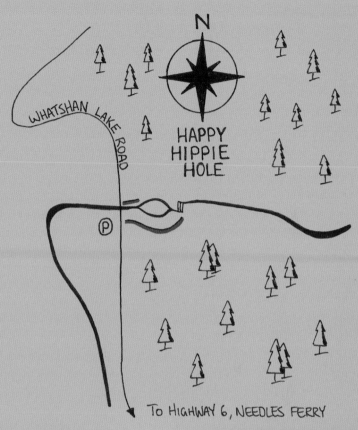

WHATSHAN LAKE ROAD

N

HAPPY
HIPPIE
HOLE

Ⓟ

TO HIGHWAY 6, NEEDLES FERRY

19. Boundary Falls

LOCATION: Greenwood
DRIVING DIFFICULTY: Easy
HIKING DIFFICULTY: Easy
HIKING DISTANCE: 300 m
HIKING TIME: 5 min.

Just when you started to think "there's gotta be a waterfall around here somewhere," Mother Nature comes through in the clutch. Halfway between the villages of Greenwood and Midway, Boundary Creek takes a sharp nosedive off a large cliff. Most people are unaware of its existence as they commute between the West Kootenays and the Okanagan on Highway 3, but they would do well to get out at this point to stretch their legs. The bird's-eye view of the waterfall from the plateau above is worth the pit stop!

Driving directions

From the visitor centre in the village of Greenwood, drive 6.5 km west on Highway 3 to a Point of Interest sign on the south side of the highway. Turn left into the parking area.

Hiking directions

From the parking area, numerous trails head west along a treed plateau high above Boundary Creek. There are many places along the plateau that look down on the creek and the waterfall. The best viewpoint is about 100 m downstream of the cascade and looks back towards the waterfall. Exercise caution, as some of the viewpoints are quite exposed, with steep drops to the creek below.

BOLTZ RD

BUTTE ST

BOUNDARY SMELTER RD

SANSON RD

To MIDWAY, OSOYOOS

Highway 3

To GREENWOOD, GRAND FORKS

N

BOUNDARY FALLS

20. *Fisherman Creek Falls*

LOCATION: Grand Forks
DRIVING DIFFICULTY: Easy
HIKING DIFFICULTY: Easy
HIKING DISTANCE: 2.5 km
HIKING TIME: 1 hr.

Fisherman Creek Falls is a small waterfall hidden in the hills above Grand Forks. There are numerous routes and trails that can be used to access the falls, as it is located just off the Trans Canada Trail. Best to set your sights on this one in the spring or early summer, as it nearly runs dry later in the season, especially in hot or dry years.

Driving directions

From the junction of Highway 3 and North Fork Road in Grand Forks, drive 10.6 km along North Fork Road. Turn left onto Old North Fork Road. Continue for 800 m to the junction with Fisherman Creek Road (small white sign in trees). Park in a small pullout at the intersection of the two roads.

Note: It is possible with a high-clearance vehicle to drive up Fisherman Creek Road a ways. Or just enjoy the walk.

Hiking directions

From the junction of Old North Fork and Fisherman Creek Road, walk up the rough road. After about 20 minutes (1 km), stay right. The road steepens for the next kilometre until it reaches a three-way intersection and a Trans Canada Trail kiosk. Go through a small wooden gate near the kiosk and follow a boot-beaten trail to the base of a tiny waterfall hidden in the forest.

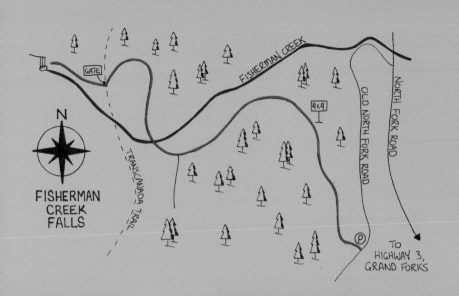

FISHERMAN
CREEK
FALLS

21. Cascade Falls

LOCATION: Christina Lake
DRIVING DIFFICULTY: Easy
HIKING DIFFICULTY: Easy
HIKING DISTANCE: 500 m
HIKING TIME: 15 min.

Driving directions

From Christina Lake, drive west on Highway 3 to its junction with Highway 395, which goes to the US border. Continue about 200 m past the intersection and turn into an unmarked pullout on the left-hand side (large "welcome to Christina Lake" sign). Just below the sign and down a dirt road is a parking area.

Hiking directions

From the parking area below the welcome sign, walk down a rough dirt road (vehicles not recommended) and past an outhouse on the left. Take the large pathway to the left of the outhouse and cross a bridge over the Kettle River. A few hundred metres past the bridge there is a yellow sign on the left side of the path. Drop off the main pathway and pick up boot-beaten trails which lead to the various vantage points above the gorge.

For a better view of the falls, return to the main trail and continue downstream with the river on your left. Trails leave the main pathway and lead to large rocky slabs high above offering a great vantage point of the water surging through a narrowing in the canyon. The trail along the Kettle River is a perfect place to stretch your legs while taking a break from travelling on Highway 3 to or from the Okanagan.

Alternatively, Cascade Falls can be accessed by heading south on Highway 395 for 1 km, parking in a pullout on the right-hand side and climbing the staircase to the trail.

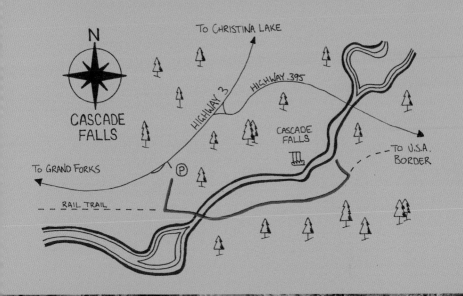

N

CASCADE FALLS

TO CHRISTINA LAKE

HIGHWAY 3

HIGHWAY 395

CASCADE FALLS

TO GRAND FORKS

TO U.S.A. BORDER

Ⓟ

RAIL TRAIL

CHAPTER 5

More To Explore

The waterfalls described in this guidebook are by no means an exhaustive list of all the cascades in the region. While this book was designed primarily with families in mind, there are many more opportunities to venture into the countless drainages, valleys and watersheds in British Columbia's mountain ranges. Have fun exploring!

A few additional waterfalls, which are recognizable to some, have been omitted due to overly lengthy approaches, excessive bushwhacking, or trail closures at the time of writing. Brief descriptions of these are included below.

1. TOBY FALLS – PURCELL WILDERNESS CONSERVANCY PROVINCIAL PARK, INVERMERE

From the town of Invermere in the East Kootenays, drive past Panorama and follow the Toby Creek Forestry Service Road to its junction with the Jumbo Creek Forestry Service Road. Near the junction of the two roads, there is a large parking area on the left for the signed Earl Grey Pass trail, complete with trailhead kiosks, a couple of campsites and an outhouse.

From the Earl Grey Pass trailhead it is approximately 14 km one way to an unsigned fork in the trail which ends near the base of the immense waterfall draining Toby Glacier. Views of the massive waterfall can be seen en route. The trail occasionally becomes overgrown with alder in avalanche paths. There are a few opportunities to camp along the way. The Earl Grey Pass trail bisects the Purcell Mountains and is often enjoyed (or not!) as a four- or five-day backpacking trip with its western trailhead near Argenta on Kootenay Lake. The logistics of having vehicles at both trailheads can be complicated.

2. FORSTER CREEK FALLS – RADIUM

Forster Creek Falls is located up the Forster Creek Forestry Service Road west of Radium in the East Kootenays. The road becomes increasingly rough and rutted with loose rocks towards the end of the road. Park in an unsigned turnaround at the very end of the road, which is used to access the Forster Meadows and Thunderwater Lake Trails.

From the parking area, cross the bridge and follow a steep gravel ATV road for a few hundred metres. When the road switches back to the left the creek can be heard roaring to the right. Look for a faint trail (typically marked by a cairn) on the right which ducks into the trees. The trail leads to a lookout for the tall waterfall.

3. OTTERTAIL FALLS – YOHO NATIONAL PARK, FIELD

If you fancy really long walks in the forest with no objective of significance, Ottertail Falls is the hike for you. From Field, drive west for 8.2 km to a small parking area on the south side of the Trans-Canada Highway. The Ottertail Valley trail connects with Goodsir Pass and the Rockwall Trail. From the trailhead it is 14.9 km to the backcountry campground at McArthur Creek. Ottertail Falls is another 2.8 km beyond the campground. You can shorten the time by biking to the McArthur Creek campground.

4. FOSTHALL FALLS – UPPER ARROW LAKE

Fosthall Falls could be the one of the most remote and arduous waterfalls to access in the Southern Interior. It is located northwest of Nakusp on the west side of Upper Arrow Lake, a looooong drive on forestry roads up the west shore. From Nakusp, drive south on Highway 23 and Highway 6 to the Arrow Park cable ferry. Cross the lake and turn right, onto Saddle Mountain Road. Follow the main Saddle Mountain Road for about 36 km to a junction and a small clearing on the right-hand side. From here Fosthall Creek is to the north, the falls to the northeast. Alternatively, you can paddle across Upper Arrow Lake to Fosthall Point and then hike along the creek to Fosthall Falls. Fosthall Creek and the multi-tiered waterfall are occasionally run by skilled kayakers.

5. EVANS CREEK FALLS AND NEMO FALLS – VALHALLA PROVINCIAL PARK, SLOCAN LAKE

These two waterfalls are located along the west shore of Slocan Lake and are accessed by canoe or kayak. The lake is nearly 40 km long and most parties take five days to paddle the shoreline, which forms the eastern boundary of Valhalla Provincial Park. There are eight well-equipped camping areas along the paddling route, with hiking trails to various highlights along the way, including Evans Creek and Nemo Falls.

6. GORGE CREEK FALLS – CRAIGELLACHIE

The trail to Cedar, Fir and Hemlock falls is currently closed due to numerous hazards, including downed trees, missing or damaged bridges and a general state of disrepair. No timeline has yet been announced for Recreation Sites and Trails BC to repair the trail. However, if and when it is reopened, the trail to this trio of waterfalls is located across the Trans-Canada Highway from The Last Spike historic site at Craigellachie, east of Sicamous.

Author's Picks

FAVOURITES

Margaret Falls, Salmon Arm
Tulip Falls, Castlegar
Twin Falls, Yoho National Park

BEST SWIMMING HOLES

Cayuse Creek Waterslide, Castlegar
Happy Hippie Hole, Farquier
Corn Creek Falls, Creston

BEST DRIVE-UP WATERFALLS (LESS THAN FIVE MINUTES)

Ione Falls, Nakusp
Sutherland Falls, Revelstoke
Marysville Falls, Kimberley

BEST PICNIC AREAS

Cottonwood Falls, Nelson
Ione Falls, Nakusp
Cherry Creek Falls, Kimberley

BEST "STROLLERABLE" FALLS

Sutherland Falls, Revelstoke
Hardy Falls, Peachland
Takakkaw Falls, Yoho National Park

BEST PLACES TO GET WET

Wapta Falls, Yoho National Park
Wilson Falls, New Denver
Rainbow Falls, Monashee Provincial Park

BEST PLACES TO SPEND A NIGHT

Little Yoho Campground, Yoho National Park
Elk Lakes Campground, Elk Lake Provincial Park
Pingston Falls, Revelstoke

Notes

1 See "Fernie Derrick" at *Fernie.com: Everything Fernie*, accessed 2020-12-12 at is.gd/VnodWn.

2 See "Morrissey" at *Ghost Towns of British Columbia*, accessed 2020-12-15 at is.gd/u46poj.

3 See "Underground for Four Generations," *Mining & Energy*, 2011-09-02, accessed 2020-12-15 at is.gd/aMEziZ.

4 See "The Railway," posted 2015-10-25 at *Off the Beaten Path with Chris and Connie*, accessed 2020-12-12 at is.gd/Aud1lA.

5 See "Backcountry lodge operator of 57 years gets one last season to run historic Yoho site," CBC News 2019-07-16, accessed 2020-12-12 at is.gd/1iR535

Resources

Recreation Sites and Trails, BC
www.sitesandtrailsbc.ca/default.aspx

BC Provincial Parks
www.env.gov.bc.ca/bcparks/

Parks Canada
www.pc.gc.ca/en/index

Alpine Club of Canada
www.alpineclubofcanada.ca/web

Drive BC
https://drivebc.ca/

Destination BC
www.hellobc.com/

Index of Waterfalls